This Anglican Church

of Ours

This Anglican Church of Ours

PATRICIA BAYS

Editor: Ellen Turnbull
Cover design: Verena Velten
Interior design and prepress production: Margaret Kyle
Proofreader: Dianne Greenslade

WoodLake is an imprint of Wood Lake Publishing, Inc. Wood Lake Publishing acknowledges the financial support of the Government of Canada, through the Book Publishing Industry Development Program (BPIDP) for its publishing activities. Wood Lake Publishing also acknowledges the financial support of the Province of British Columbia through the Book Publishing Tax Credit.

BNC CERTIFIED | **BIBLIOGRAPHIC DATA 2011-12**

At Wood Lake Publishing, we practise what we publish, being guided by a concern for fairness, justice, and equal opportunity in all of our relationships with employees and customers. Wood Lake Publishing is committed to caring for the environment and all creation. Wood Lake Publishing recycles, reuses, and encourages readers to do the same. Resources are printed on 100% post-consumer recycled paper and more environmentally friendly groundwood papers (newsprint), whenever possible. A percentage of all profit is donated to charitable organizations.

Library and Archives Canada Cataloguing in Publication
Bays, Patricia
   This Anglican Church of ours / Patricia Bays. – Rev. and updated ed.
Includes bibliographical references.
ISBN 978-1-77064-439-7
   1. Anglican Church of Canada. I. Title.
BX5614.B39 2012   283'.71   C2012-900600-9

Published by WoodLake
An imprint of Wood Lake Publishing Inc.
9590 Jim Bailey Road, Kelowna, BC, Canada, V4V 1R2
www.woodlakebooks.com
250.766.2778

Printing 10 9 8 7 6 5 4 3 2 1
Printed in Canada by
Houghton Boston

Contents

Foreword

Foreword to the First Edition by Michael Peers

If you are a newcomer trying to find your way into the Anglican Church, or perhaps returning from a time away, or simply looking for a helpful handbook to our church, then you have found the right guide. I have known Patricia Bays since student days, and recognize in her book both the depth of scholarship and the breadth of interest that I remember from those years.

Patricia begins by sharing her own story of her journey into Anglicanism. It is personal, real, inviting, and honest. As you read it, you realize you are coming to know a woman who loves her church, and who is pleased to offer the reader a deeper knowledge of it. In the end, I suspect that is how we come to any involvement in the life of the church – through someone whose own engagement touches us. When, later in the book, Patricia describes evangelism as a ministry of hospitality, we know we are in the hands of someone who practices what she preaches. Her own welcome of us into her experience of the life of the church serves to help us trust her as a guide.

Perhaps Patricia's commitment to her vocation as an educator makes her such a good storyteller. She has a gift for taking complex concerns and issues, and making them available to her readers. In writing of the origins and tracing the tale of Anglicanism, she is able to touch key moments and open them up in a way that allows us to lay hold of the heart of them. When she shares basic information, such as the government or structures of our church at its different levels, her explanations are simple and clear. Bewildering church "jargon" is unveiled and rendered intelligible – not an easy task! Patricia has an ability to explain the mystery of Anglican life and worship, and at the same time help us become aware of the deeper mystery of our faith in God and God's love.

A section of the book that I especially treasure is the chapter on Anglican theology. It is well titled: "Is there an Anglican theology?" And the question is wonderfully explored. She is wise to say that since theology is a word about God, "…a word that we are all saying every day of our lives… something that deeply affects each of us," then it is "far too important to be left to the clergy or the professional theologians." I respond with a hearty "Yes!" It is in partnership, in the sharing of our experience of God one with another, in reflecting on our worship and prayer and its connection with the truth of our lives, that theology becomes a living, vital reality. The best theology is done not in classrooms – as important as that is – but in our homes and workplaces. Patricia does not denigrate the place of scholars, but she pushes us to repossess the study of theology as a task for the whole church. An "Anglican theology" is a theology done by Anglicans as they reflect on God in all aspects of their lives.

But there is another aspect that I also appreciate. She writes: "Our style of theological discourse reflects our acceptance of the world as a place of ambiguity, a place for ongoing exploration of what faith means when lived in such a world." She recognizes that our penchant for living with this ambiguity, and our resistance to doctrinal precision, leaves us open to the charge of being sloppy and careless. But she reveals her true Anglican spirit when she refuses to be trapped by that charge!

There are themes here that are not normally developed in such books: a fine piece on stewardship that takes as a starting point the generosity and self-giving of God in creation; chapters on our ministry as a gathered people and as individuals, ethical decision-making, and ecumenism; and, as I mentioned earlier, a chapter on the nature and practice of evangelism. I praise Patricia's willingness to tackle some hard issues with which our church is wrestling today.

Like any good story, this one looks ahead to the challenges of the future. God's church is a living community with a past and a present – but the story continues. Not all has been written: there is much to come. What Patricia Bays *has* written, with affection and openness, is a wonderful road map for any who are already travelling an Anglican path, and for those who wish to explore it. I am grateful for this timely contribution to the story of the Anglican Church of Canada.

Michael Peers
Primate, The Anglican Church of Canada

Foreword to This Edition by Fred Hiltz

With so many others I welcome the update of *This Anglican Church of Ours* by Patricia Bays. It is an excellent overview of a church whose heart beats with a deep desire to proclaim the gospel through beautiful liturgy and loving outreach; in tending the suffering and working for peace and justice; and in caring for the earth, stewarding its resources for the benefit of generations to come.

Bays paints a picture of a church whose local witness in every parish is of distinct value, lending its own colour and hue to the mosaic of The Anglican Church of Canada and the yet broader canvas of the Anglican Communion and its commitment to God's mission in the world. It sparkles with the essence of who Anglicans are and how we strive to be faithful servants of Christ with the gospel he has entrusted to the church.

For many pastors it's a book we will keep within easy reach for quick reference in speaking to someone on the phone, in responding to an e-mail inquiry, or in a conversation over a coffee.

The book is a gem. It's informative, inspiring, and inviting. It's a wonderful introduction for those who may be exploring Christian faith in general and the Anglican tradition in particular. It's an excellent resource for catechesis – for preparing men and women for baptism and confirmation. It's a superb guide for those seeking reception into The Anglican Church of Canada. And for the rest of us, it's a succinct refresher course in the spirit, ethos, and polity of being Christian in the Anglican way.

In her own scholarly and pastoral way, Bays has touched the lives of hundreds of men and women and played a significant role in their decision to join The Anglican Church of Canada and in their abiding commitment to its life and witness.

Thank you, Patricia, for being such a wise and gracious ambassador for our beloved Church.

Fred Hiltz
Primate, The Anglican Church of Canada

Preface

Preface to the First Edition

One of the characteristics of Anglicanism is its diversity. Anglicans hold a variety of views on a subject. So, in this book, you will find a personal view of the Anglican Church, and Anglican theology and customs. I hope that you will recognize in it Anglican churches you have attended or visited. Undoubtedly some Anglicans will disagree with what is here. The next book will be up to them!

I want to offer my deep appreciation to all who have assisted with the writing of this book:

- Michelle Bax and Marilyn Dean, who read the manuscript and made suggestions, and Barbara-Lynn Dixon who raised the questions.
- Laurel Ayerst for her contribution on Stewardship, and Dennis Cluely (Brotherhood of Anglican Churchmen) and Joan Peterson (Mothers' Union) for information about their organizations.
- Archdeacon William Portman of the Diocese of Qu'Appelle and Dorothy Kealey of the Archives of General Synod who contributed material.
- Patrick Tomalin, Karen Evans, and Vianney (Sam) Carriere for help with photographs.
- Jim Taylor, Mike Schwartzentruber, and the staff at Wood Lake Books for bringing the manuscript to publication.
- Finally, and most importantly, Eric, Jonathan, and Becky who read the work in progress, contributed ideas and cheered me up when the project seemed impossible!

Thank you to everyone.

Patricia Bays

Preface to This Edition

I am honoured and touched by the way the book has been received in the life of our church. I hear from many Anglicans in many parts of the country that it has been helpful for them in coming to understand our church.

Much has changed in the lives of the Anglican Church of Canada and the Anglican Communion in the 17 years since this book was first published. This new edition brings the story up to date.

My thanks to those who helped with information and support:

- Judy Steers of the national office, Lisa Chisholm-Smith, and the Ven. Susan Churchill-Lackey of the Diocese of Ottawa.
- David Jones and Catrina Tapley, for their contribution about stewardship.
- Mike Schwartzentruber, Ellen Turnbull, and the staff at Wood Lake Publishing for bringing the manuscript to production.
- Jim Taylor for the original study guide, now updated.
- And, as ever, my family for their love and support.

Patricia Bays

Introduction

Many years ago a collection of essays with the title *They Became Anglicans* was written by a number of well-known Anglicans who had formerly been members of other churches. They wrote about why they chose the Anglican Church.

There is a new emphasis in Christianity on storytelling. Storytelling lets us understand ourselves and our journey better; story listening lets us hear and understand others. I hope that this book will encourage you to explore your own story and to see how it connects (or not) with the church's story.

My story

I was born the oldest child of a Scottish Presbyterian mother and an Irish Roman Catholic father, and baptized and raised in the Roman Catholic Church. Our regular Sunday attendance at Mass was so much the norm that I think I can count the few Sundays that I missed church. Religious customs were a part of everyday life. We were the only family who left the summer cottage in our Sunday best (hats and white gloves!) to drive to church. We recited the family rosary, said grace at meals, fasted on Fridays, and went to church schools. As Roman Catholics in Protestant Ontario, we felt ourselves part of a minority and we preserved our specialness by our faithful observance of traditions. In church, I felt a strong sense of belonging and security, and a deep enjoyment of the mystery of worship.

My Presbyterian grandmother lived with us. She demanded very strict standards of behaviour from us – no noisy games on Sunday was the rule I remember best – and was given to singing evangelistic hymns in the kitchen.

I learned Bible stories and hymns from her, along with a sense of God as a very strict parent (a view that I struggled for many years to overcome).

For grades 5 to 13, my sister and I attended the Ontario Ladies' College, a United Church girls' school in our hometown of Whitby. It was one of the most formative influences in my life, not only for its emphasis on academic excellence and musical education, but also for its contribution to my religious journey. It was a school shaped by the Christian tradition. The principal, the Rev. Dr. Stanley Osborne, was a fine musician and an accomplished theologian. His Christian knowledge classes gave us current scholarship in biblical and theological subjects and were an excellent introduction to my later studies.

My mother was refused Communion in the Roman Catholic Church because she sent us to a Protestant school, so she decided to attend the Anglican Church as a middle road. I remember my terror at first entering an Anglican church; I was sure that the Pope would find out! My sister and I were immediately drawn to the music of the liturgy and to the prospect of singing in the choir. In this tiny parish, the arrival of three new singers was cause for celebration.

St. John's Port Whitby was a very different sort of church for me. In the evangelical tradition of Anglicanism, St. John's had a simple and unadorned style of worship, and monthly celebrations of the Holy Communion. I had to learn my way around the Prayer Book and the new hymns and canticles, and adjust to the idea of longer sermons! I embraced it all with enthusiasm – the extrovert always ready to join a new group. I felt welcomed and needed by the parish and I was missed if I was not there.

After grade 13, I enrolled in Trinity College at the University of Toronto. Here I found a different Anglican world. The Prayer Book was the same. I learned new hymns but still knew my way around the services. But the liturgical practice was very different, much more like the Roman Catholic tradition of my childhood. The priest wore coloured Eucharistic vestments and celebrated the Eucharist facing the altar with his back to the congregation. People genuflected, made the sign of the cross, went to sacramental confession, went on retreats. The Eucharist was celebrated daily.

Here the many different parts of my religious experience began to come together – the love of ritual and colour and mystery of my early days, and the hymns and Scripture and active participation of my more recent Anglican experience.

At the same time, I began the study of English literature; a love which continues to this day. For me, fiction, poetry and drama are ways in which I come to know God and to reflect on our quest for meaning in life. A current interest of mine is using literature in religious education, to encourage the use of imagination in exploring the Christian faith.

At Trinity, I sang in the chapel choir, worshipped regularly in the chapel, participated in the life of the Anglican community, and took the four compulsory religious knowledge courses. They ranged from biblical and theological subjects to existentialism. Those years of compulsory religious knowledge classes in university resulted in a whole generation of community leaders and captains of industry in Canada who are literate in the Christian faith. For the sake of our national life and culture, I am sorry that requirement is gone.

At the end of my Arts course, I decided to enroll in the faculty of divinity. The ordination of women was not even thought of in those days, so the few women who studied theology did so from academic interest and love of the subject rather than from any clear idea of what jobs in the church might look like. There were only three women in my divinity class. This was a formative time: to study biblical and theological subjects in depth, to explore the Christian faith, to develop habits of worship.

The early 1960s were heady times. The Roman Catholic Council Vatican II opened up opportunities for discussion between Anglicans and that church. The new trends in liturgy, new understandings in pastoral theology, and new approaches in education and lay training were exciting. The Anglican Congress in Toronto in 1963 brought Anglicans from all over the world right into our college dining room and heightened our awareness of our membership in a worldwide family. As a summer student, I worked at our national church office helping to write what was known for the next 20 years as "the new curriculum," an innovative process-centred approach to Sunday school teaching.

After graduation, I worked in Winnipeg as a parish director of Christian Education. I was married there to Eric, who was a parish priest. Our two children were born in Winnipeg and we learned what it meant to be a clergy family.

We moved to Saskatoon where Eric and I both taught at the seminary, the College of Emmanuel and St. Chad. This gave us another view of the Anglican Church, seen through the lens of ministry training. My husband became the Bishop of Qu'Appelle, a diocese in southern Saskatchewan, and this gave me yet another perspective, the world of diocesan life.

From 1968 until 2007, I was involved with the life of the Anglican Church of Canada at the national level. I have been on national committees that looked at ecumenism, at mission, at doctrine and worship. I have written curriculum materials used by many parishes and travelled all over Canada doing leadership training workshops of one sort or another. I have also had the privilege of representing the Anglican Church of Canada at international gatherings.

So my life as a member of this church has brought me a great diversity and richness of experience.

I enjoy opportunities to work and pray with Christians of other denominations and am committed to the search for unity. I can see some of the shortcomings in the life of the Anglican community. But I love the Anglican Church and am committed to living and working within this family.

What I love about the Anglican church

I love the worship, with its ordered patterns of prayer, the same from week to week and yet varied according to the seasons. I love the rhythm and music of the language of worship. Anglican worship is full of colour, dramatic action, sometimes the smell of incense, and music from a rich tradition.

I appreciate also a certain "matter of factness" about Anglican worship. We join in common prayer. We join together in the worship of God according to our accustomed patterns.

The sacraments, particularly the Eucharist, are important for me too. The Eucharist is daily bread, food for our journey, something which sustains us as we share in it. It is to be celebrated frequently and on all occasions, in sorrow as well as in joy.

The Anglican Church has a fine intellectual tradition and values theological exploration. So I appreciate the freedom to question and explore what the church offers. I love also the Anglican encouragement for the life of the imagination. I want to be able to find God through art and music and fiction and poetry.

The growth of a very dark theology in some denominations today puzzles me. This theology says that the world is evil, that human beings are sinful, that we need to separate ourselves from this world. The Anglican position affirms that the world and human beings are good because they are God's creation. We must work to bring all of humanity to its full potential as God intended, and I rejoice that we do this by being involved in our society.

I like the diversity that Anglicanism offers. Within our communion we have a variety of styles of worship and theological emphases, and I believe that our strength lies in this diversity. We try to balance order and flexibility by not defining things too closely. Yet we maintain a strong sense of family, of connections, of links in worship and structure.

Of course, many of these factors are to be found in other denominations too, and we each have our own reasons for membership. I invite you to join with me in exploring what the Anglican Church and Anglicans are like.

About this book

For some of you reading this book, everything I have said so far will be familiar. For others, perhaps newcomers to the Anglican Church, some of this may be new.

Every reader will be at a different stage of familiarity with this church. For that reason, I have arranged the chapters according to the amount of detail that readers may be willing to digest. That is, the opening chapters are a fairly basic description of who Anglicans are, and how we got that way. The later chapters move into more detail. For those who already have some familiarity with the Anglican Church, they may become a reference source. The book contains a glossary of terms for easy reference.

You don't have to read this book in the order it has been printed. You don't even have to read all of the book. But I hope that, however much you read, you will find that as a result you too end up falling in love with this Anglican Church of ours.

1

Who are the Anglicans?

Anglicans are members of a worldwide family of churches. We trace our descent from the church in England.

In 1984, I visited the cathedral in Lagos, Nigeria. A choir of men and boys wearing maroon cassocks and white surplices sang the traditional service of Evensong from *The Book of Common Prayer*. When I closed my eyes, I easily imagined myself in an English cathedral. But when I opened them, I could see the afternoon sun through open windows. I could smell the spices of Africa and feel the traffic noise from the square outside.

Later in my trip I went to a Nigerian village. There, the music was African, and the language strange to me, yet I knew exactly what was going on as we moved through the familiar service. This village was proud of the fact that they had received the message of the gospel not through foreign missionaries but through their own members who had travelled to the coast and been baptized there. The welcome I received as a fellow Anglican was deeply moving.

From 1981 to 1987, I was the lay member for Canada on the Anglican Consultative Council and I visited Anglican churches in many other countries. Here are some journal excerpts that describe some varieties of Anglican worship that I encountered.

Isonin, Nigeria, July 21, 1984

As we get out of the car, the Women's Guild pour out of the church, singing songs of welcome. I feel overwhelmed, surrounded by these smiling, dancing figures. The music is loud and rhythmical, accompanied by clapping and strong melodies. I am escorted into church by this singing band and, once inside, the ladies sing songs and hymns for about 15 minutes.

The service is shortened – Mattins in the Yoruba language. I have the music to the responses and am able to tell roughly where we are. I sing the hymns in English. There are drums and sticks as well as the organ, and people sway to the rhythm of the very Western hymn tunes. I give the sermon, which is interpreted paragraph by paragraph. I recognize the words "Mrs. Patricia Bays" used frequently throughout the announcements and prayers. Here is African music with clapping, dancing, arm-waving. It is exciting to watch and share their joy in the music. Between each song, the leader cries "Fellowship," to which the reply is, "In Jesus Christ."

The church is packed. Most people are in local dress. Every woman but me has her head covered with a wrapped headdress or hat.

Kyoto, Japan, May 10, 1987

By taxi to church – very English in its appearance and very "catholic" in its manner – six candles, servers in cottas, Sarum bows and the works. First there is Mattins, then the Eucharist. Although the service is all in Japanese, the pattern of the service is recognizable from the actions. I sing the Easter hymns in English and nobody seems to notice. After the service, while the announcements are being made, the women of the congregation serve seaweed tea in small handle-less cups.

Madrid, Spain, October 25, 1987

Along with other Anglicans, I visited the Spanish Reformed Episcopal Church, now a part of the Anglican Communion. The church is tucked away between large buildings, its façade indistinguishable except for the letters over the door. There is no stained glass, but painted on the walls are many biblical verses.

The service is very Anglican. The bishop wears the ordinary dress of a priest except for his purple shirt. At communion, the front pew is filled with those next in line for communion; when the rail is empty, they all go forward as a group, receive communion and, after a signal from the bishop, stand and leave as a group.

Our diocese of Qu'Appelle had a companion relationship with the Diocese of West Malaysia, and Eric and I visited that diocese on two occasions. We had an opportunity to visit many Tamil and Chinese churches, and were overwhelmed by the warm hospitality of our Anglican brothers and sisters.

Kuala Lumpur, Malaysia, January 9, 1993

The wedding of the Rev. Franklin Benjamin and Margaret Victor. There was a large Tamil congregation, the women all in saris. The bride wore a red and gold sari with a cathedral train that extended half the length of the church and a white floral band and face veil. Both the bride and groom wore traditional garlands of cream flowers. Rings had been exchanged at the time of betrothal. At this wedding service, a special gold necklace was blessed by the bishop and received by the bride. The hymns and liturgy were in Tamil, though we sang the psalm to Anglican chant and sang "O Perfect Love."

Carey Island, Malaysia, January 24, 1994

We drove to a large oil palm plantation over red gravel roads, passing mile after mile of oil palms planted in straight rows. In a clearing, there was a small village of houses and a small frame church with a tin roof. We sat on benches; the heat was incredible. The music was provided by a guitarist and two small boys in orange shirts who played a lively beat on the drums. Outside, a young boy watched a flock of tiny goats. He edged nearer and nearer to the open windows of the church as he tried to hear what was going on inside.

I also remember:

- The ordination of a locally raised-up deacon in one church of a rural multipoint parish in New Zealand, where the parish was struggling to discover what forms ministry might take when stipendiary clergy could no longer be paid.
- The splendid service celebrating the 700th anniversary of the building of the Angel Choir at Lincoln Cathedral in England, with the Queen and Prince Philip in attendance.
- The Toronto congregation with mainly Ugandan members.
- The small church sitting in an open field under the vast prairie sky.

Everywhere there has been a warm welcome for a fellow Anglican, and I felt at home as the familiar words or actions of the service unfolded. I can never sing the hymn, "The day thou gavest, Lord, is ended" (in *Common Praise*, #29) without being moved by its description of the worldwide church.

> *As o'er each continent and island*
> *The dawn leads on another day,*
> *The voice of prayer is never silent,*
> *Nor dies the strain of praise away.*

As we go to sleep each night, other Christians are waking to pray. A chain of prayer links the members of our worldwide family.

The spread of Anglicanism around the world

As I mentioned in the introduction, Anglicanism travelled on the coattails of the British Empire. As British ships, traders, and armies penetrated all parts of the world, they opened up opportunities for the church to travel with them.

The first recorded Anglican Eucharist in North America was celebrated in Frobisher Bay in 1578 by Robert Wolfall, chaplain to Martin Frobisher's expedition in search of the fabled Northwest Passage to the Orient. In the Calendar of *The Book of Common Prayer* (*BCP*), we commemorate this event on September 3.

As the British settled in the Thirteen Colonies, in what was to become the United States, Anglican clergy accompanied them and helped to establish parish life along the eastern seaboard. As the British began to settle in Canada, Anglicans came to the Maritimes and Upper and Lower Canada, and missionaries ventured out to the Red River and along the fur trade routes.

The first Anglican bishop in Canada, Charles Inglis, was consecrated on August 12, 1787, as "Bishop of Nova Scotia and its dependencies." His arrival established the Church of England in a colony loyal to Britain. Inglis' territory was huge, but it was some years before other dioceses were created: the Diocese of Quebec in 1793, the Dioceses of Toronto and Newfoundland in 1839, the Diocese of Fredericton in 1845, the Diocese of Rupert's Land in 1849.

Among the very early Anglicans in Canada were Chief Joseph Brant and his people of the Six Nations. The Chapel Royal of the Mohawks was built in 1713, near what is now the city of Brantford, Ontario.

Australia, New Zealand, and the Caribbean, as former British colonies, have similar histories to Canada. In the nineteenth century, missionaries travelled to Africa, Asia, and Latin America, setting up Anglican churches. These churches for many years were governed by English bishops and followed patterns of life similar to those in England. Now national churches have indigenous leadership and their customs, language, and traditions reflect the culture of the land.

At one time, *The Book of Common Prayer* was used in all Anglican churches, and the traveller used the same words in every country. This phase was followed by revisions that made it more suited to the local culture. Some of these revisions were in languages other than English. Now the modern-language liturgies all follow a similar pattern, because of the worldwide movement for liturgical renewal. So, when visiting churches in Australia, New Zealand, South Africa, or the United States, we still are aware that we are participating in a liturgy that is familiar to us. When our son went as a volunteer to Western Samoa, he sought out the Anglican Church in Apia. It gave him a church community of which he felt a part while he was far from home.

As members of the Anglican Church of Canada, we belong to the Anglican Communion. The name suggests our historical roots in the Church of England, and suggests also the close relationship and "bonds of affection" that we share. We are more than a collection of independent churches. We belong to a common family, enriched by our interconnectedness. (For more detail about the structure and organization of the Anglican Church, see Chapter 17.)

Our common characteristics

Anglicans live in many parts of the world, speak many languages, and have many different customs. What then do we have in common? I believe that a number of characteristics define us as Anglicans, even though language and traditions may vary.

We share a common history and a common pattern of worship. Our life as a church centres on the importance of common prayer and liturgy. The Anglican Church is not a "confessional" church that subscribes to a set of beliefs written down in a confessional statement. Anglican belief is recorded in the words of the liturgy. For example, prayers for the Baptismal service say what Anglicans believe about Baptism. What we believe about the Eucharist is contained in the words of the Communion service.

We use books of prayers as we join together in "common prayer" and these books form the centre of our common life in the church. Today the words may also be found in leaflets or projected onto screens. But the words are the familiar liturgies found in our prayer books. Many people who have become Anglican from other backgrounds speak of the liturgy, the forms of worship, as the factor which attracted them to the Anglican Church.

The Anglican approach to theology is based on the doctrines of Creation and Incarnation. We believe that God created the world, and that the world is good. We believe that human beings, male and female, are part of God's good creation. We believe that God's good creation has been marred by human selfishness and an unwillingness to seek and follow divine will. We believe that God chose to come into this world in human form, and that God redeemed the world through the death and resurrection of Jesus. We believe that God continues to be active in the world, both in the work of creation and in the work of restoration to wholeness.

So Anglicans believe that it is right for us to be involved in social and political action in order to make our society a place in which all can flourish and grow. Because God is active in the world today, we have a responsibility to care for others. Anglicans have historically been active in government, social agencies, and community institutions. Our prayers, in *The Book of Common Prayer (BCP)* and in *The Book of Alternative Services (BAS)*, remind us of our concern for political order and process, and our concern for the needs of the world. We do not separate ourselves from the world but work within its structures to bring justice and wholeness to all. This is not just a whim or a fad but is grounded in our theological belief in the Incarnation – God's choice to be fully revealed as a human being, whom we know as Jesus of Nazareth.

Anglicans share a common form of church government. Our forms of ordained ministry are bishop, priest, and deacon (see Chapter 16). The Catechism in the American *Book of Common Prayer* speaks of four orders of ministry: laity, deacons, priests, and bishops. The fourth order emphasizes that the laity, the people of God, are **all** called to ministry.

Our life is organized in dioceses, regional groupings of parishes each headed by a bishop (*episcopos*) who has the responsibility for the oversight (*episcope*) of the life of the Church in that area. Clergy and laity meet in synods, gatherings held to make decisions about the life of the Anglican Church. So our form of government is a combination of episcopal authority and parliamentary democracy.

Perhaps the most noticeable characteristic of Anglicanism is its acceptance of variety and diversity. Throughout our history we have tried to hold together in one church a variety of theological perspectives and liturgical practices. Because we do not have a list of beliefs written down in a "confession of faith," we have been able to include this diversity within our liturgies. Services range from simple, with little ornament or gesture, to elaborate, complete with the Eucharist, incense, vestments, music, and ceremonial.

This acceptance of diversity has enabled our Church to adapt to local culture and customs. But it sometimes makes us difficult to define. The Presbyterian theologian Elizabeth Templeton, in speaking to the Lambeth Conference in 1988, said of the Anglican Church, "Both internally and in relation to other evolving Christian life-forms, you have been conspicuously unclassifiable, a kind of ecclesiastical duck-billed platypus, robustly mammal and vigorously egg-laying. That, I am sure, is to be celebrated and not deplored." Our openness to diversity enables us to live as family with Christians in other parts of the world, and is a gift of the Anglican Church to the rest of the world.

As this book explores something of what it means to be an Anglican in Canada in the 21st century, we will have an opportunity to look at many issues in greater depth. And a bibliography of helpful books is on page 175.

2

What are the origins of the Anglican Church?

One of the popular misconceptions about the Anglican Church is that it came into being because of the marital problems of Henry VIII. Certainly the Church of England established its independence from Rome during the Tudor period of Henry VIII, Edward VI, and Elizabeth I. But the roots of the Anglican Church go back to the early years of Christianity in the British Isles.

The Celtic church

According to legend, Christianity arrived in Britain within the lifetimes of those who knew Jesus personally. Joseph of Arimathea, for instance, who provided his own new tomb for Jesus' burial, is linked with Glastonbury in England. Legend has it that Joseph of Arimathea was a tin merchant who travelled to England to trade with the tin mines in Cornwall. Some stories even say that Jesus was Joseph's nephew, and travelled to England with him. (This gave rise to William Blake's poem, later made into a hymn: "And did those feet in ancient time / Walk upon England's mountains green?") After Jesus' death, Joseph is said to have returned to England as a Christian missionary. At Glastonbury, he planted his staff in the ground. It took root, burst into leaf, and became the famed flowering Glastonbury thorn.

It is also likely that there were Christians among the Roman soldiers occupying Britain. The Christian religion was certainly present by 200 CE: St. Alban, the first English martyr, was killed in 209.

When the Romans left Britain around 400 CE and waves of invaders arrived, the Celtic peoples in the west and north maintained their culture and faith. Their form of Christianity grew and flourished and still influences our spirituality. The story of the Celtic church is told through the stories of its saints: Ninian, Patrick, Columba (Columcille), Brigid, Cuthbert, David, and many others. Celtic society was organized on tribal lines and governed by chiefs or kings. The Celtic church was organized around monasteries ruled by abbots. The abbeys preserved learning, instructed the young, and created beautiful works of religious art in the form of illuminated manuscripts, stone carvings, and metalwork.

There are a number of aspects of Celtic Christianity that are important to Anglican spirituality. Firstly, Celtic Christianity has a strong sense of the presence of God in everyday life. God is found and worshipped in the daily tasks. Many Celtic prayers are full of the homey details of rural life. Esther de Waal, in her book *A World Made Whole* (published by Fount, 1991) includes these Celtic prayers:

I will kindle my fire this morning
In the presence of the holy angels of heaven.

Bless O God my little cow
Bless O God my desire;
Bless thou my partnership
And the milking of my hands, O God.

This is religion of the Incarnation, reminding us that God's life – like the Celtic knot design – is closely interwoven with our human life. The hymn "St. Patrick's Breastplate" (*CP* #436) reminds us,

Christ be with me, Christ within me, Christ behind me, Christ before me,
Christ beside me, Christ to win me, Christ to comfort and restore me.

Secondly, Celtic Christianity believes in the goodness of nature. It sees humans as made in God's image, full of goodness and not intrinsically sinful. God's grace is at work in our lives. This is an optimistic view of human nature and the created world, one which fits well with our Anglican understanding of creation, incarnation, and redemption.

Celtic Christianity also has a strong sense of the communion of saints. It affirms that we are surrounded on our pilgrimage by faithful Christian men and women of earlier times. God the Trinity, the saints of old – all are near us and accessible to us in our prayers. Celtic Christianity is rich in stories and legends, in images and symbols, art and music.

Roman Christianity returned to Britain with the arrival of St. Augustine at Canterbury in 597, and the Roman tradition and form of government spread throughout England. Although Celtic Christianity was gradually eclipsed by Roman practice, many customs and traditions survived. In the last 40 years there has been renewed interest in exploring this part of our Anglican heritage.

Henry VIII and the Reformation

The 15th and 16th centuries in Europe were periods of upheaval in the church. Discontent with papal government and the abuse of church customs, combined with the availability of new translations of Scripture from Latin into local languages, produced a desire to look again at the roots of the Christian faith and return to the basics of Christian teaching. Individual figures like John Calvin, Martin Luther, Ulrich Zwingli, and John Knox promoted doctrinal and organizational reform in Europe during this time.

England knew of the work of these reformers and had the Scriptures in English through the work of William Tyndale (1526). But the church was not deeply affected by them. In fact Henry VIII, conservative in theology and practice, received from the Pope in 1521 the title "Defender of the Faith" for his paper criticizing Martin Luther.

But the King was experiencing political difficulties. His marriage of almost 20 years to the Spanish princess Catherine of Aragon produced only one living child, their daughter Mary. Increasingly anxious over the succession to the throne, Henry decided to divorce Catherine and to marry Anne Boleyn. Securing an annulment and obtaining a papal dispensation to remarry was not an impossible request. These matters had been easily resolved before. But European politics introduced a complicating factor.

Catherine's nephew was the Emperor Charles V. The Pope was being threatened by the Emperor and so could not grant Henry's request.

Henry decided then to remove the church in England from the control of foreign powers. Acts of Parliament were passed, Henry's marriage was declared invalid, and he married Anne Boleyn. The Pope promptly excommunicated Henry. Henry took increasing control of the English church, dissolving the monasteries and transferring their wealth to the crown, creating new bishoprics, and declaring himself head of the church. Although he ordered the English Bible placed in all churches, he remained very conservative in matters of religious practice. This was basically the Catholic Church without allegiance to the Pope.

Henry was succeeded in 1547 by his son Edward VI. Edward had been educated by teachers with Protestant sympathies. During his reign the church was increasingly influenced by Lutheran and Calvinist teachings. In 1549, the first *Book of Common Prayer*, drawn up by Thomas Cranmer, Archbishop of Canterbury, was authorized. The Act of Uniformity made its use mandatory in all churches in England. This book (with its revisions) has become the normative statement of Anglican theology and practice.

The 1549 book was a compromise between traditionalists and reformers, and so pleased neither. In 1552, a second *Book of Common Prayer* was issued. It followed more Protestant principles.

During the reign of Edward VI, a number of Articles were published to define the position of the Church of England as a middle way between Catholic worship and the new Calvinist reforms. In all, 42 Articles were proposed in 1552. These were not accepted but, in 1559, during the reign of Elizabeth I, the Thirty-nine Articles were adopted as a balanced statement of the Anglican position on certain disputed topics. (These are found printed in the *BCP* on pages 698–714.) They are not a formal and full statement of doctrine, but rather an attempt to deal with certain controversies of the 16th century. The articles try to avoid a narrow definition and leave room for a variety of interpretation; establishing this breadth of expression was an important principle of Anglican theology.

Edward was succeeded by his half-sister Mary, a devout Roman Catholic. As the daughter of Catherine of Aragon, Mary wanted to return England to the worship of the Roman Catholic Church. During her reign, many reformers were executed – Bishops Thomas Cranmer, Hugh Latimer, and Nicholas Ridley among them. On Mary's death, her half-sister Elizabeth became Queen. She wished to restore stability to the country and preserve England from foreign domination. This meant the church should retain its heritage but remain free of control by the Pope. The form of liturgy, the three-fold order of bishops, priests, and deacons, and the sacraments were all retained. But the services were in English, the reading of Scripture was encouraged, clergy could marry, and many of the corruptions and superstitions of the medieval church were abandoned. A third *Book of Common Prayer* was issued in 1559.

The aim of the Elizabethan church was to bring stability to both church and state, by the compromise of steering a middle way. By avoiding narrow definitions and regulations, the Church of England held together in a family with a variety of views. Richard Hooker (1554–1600) was the apologist for the emerging Anglican position. His *Treatise on the Laws of Ecclesiastical Polity* defined the Anglican approach to theology, the balance of Scripture, Tradition and Reason. He saw the church as organic and dynamic, framing its life in each era by looking at scripture and tradition in the light of reason and experience.

The Puritans and the Restoration

There were, however, Protestants dissatisfied with the Elizabethan Settlement who wished to reform the church further along Calvinist lines. They disapproved of ceremonial, and emphasized preaching. Some sought to abolish episcopacy (bishops) as a form of church government. When Oliver Cromwell established the Commonwealth in the 1640s, Puritanism dominated the religious life of England. But its strict standards caused much division and the rise of many other religious movements such as Quakers, Congregationalists, and Baptists.

When the monarchy was restored in 1660, the Church of England returned to its position as the established church. The Act of Uniformity of 1662 authorized a revised prayer book that remained the standard text for worship until the 20th century.

The 18th and 19th centuries

The 18th century was a dry period in the life of the Church of England. Clergy continued to minister within systems that had been established a couple of centuries before.

Yet the country was undergoing enormous social change. The Industrial Revolution brought many people from the country to the factories and the towns. The problem of urban poverty was great.

In 1738, an Anglican priest John Wesley had a profound conversion experience and began evangelistic work, preaching the gospel in the fields and towns of England. He went out to meet the people where they were. He attracted many followers and recruited lay preachers to assist in this work. The system of beliefs and practices became known as Methodism. Wesley wished the Methodist movement to take place within the Church of England, but the system gradually became independent. John and his brother Charles, one of the greatest of Anglican hymn writers, remained Anglican priests; but after their deaths, Methodism became separate from the Church of England, following its own pattern of government by conference, ordaining its own ministers, and administering its own sacraments. Methodism has since spread to many parts of the world.

At the same time, a similar movement, the Evangelical Revival, was taking place within the Church of England. This movement placed a new stress on personal conversion, salvation by faith in Christ's atoning death, the sole authority of Scripture, and the importance of the preaching of the Word. Influenced by evangelical clergy, the missionary movement brought the gospel to all parts of the world. At home in England, evangelicals played a major role in the abolition of slavery and the reform of social conditions.

In the 19th century, the Anglo-Catholic revival brought a new emphasis to the liturgical and sacramental life of the church. The Oxford Movement, as it became known, aimed at restoring high church ideals to the Church of England. These reformers were sometimes called Tractarians because of the writings, *Tracts for the Times*, in which they set out their views. The movement emphasized the catholic and apostolic nature of the church, looking back to its historic roots. It placed new importance on the liturgical and sacramental life of the church; the introduction of vestments, candles, ceremonial, and ritual soon followed. Anglo-Catholics were involved in ministry to the slums of large English cities, and in missionary work around the world. During this period, religious orders of monks and nuns were re-established, and continue in the Anglican Church to this day.

The 20th century

In the 19th century, the Anglican Church spread throughout the world. In the 20th century, the resulting national churches became independent Provinces, each taking responsibility for its own life but joining with fellow Anglicans to form the Anglican Communion.

Churches have developed new forms of government. Decisions affecting the life of a Province are now made by **synods** or parliaments of bishops, clergy, and lay people. The laity has begun to take a much more active role in ministry, in worship services, and in decision-making.

Liturgical renewal has taken place over almost the whole century. Anglican churches all over the world have developed contemporary liturgies in the language of the country. This liturgical renewal has been part of a worldwide movement by liturgical scholars of many denominations.

The ecumenical movement has brought the Anglican Church into dialogue with other Christians and with other world religions. Years of dialogue with the Evangelical Lutheran Church in Canada have resulted in a relationship of "full communion" with that church.

The Anglican Church continues to hold a variety of theological positions in creative tension. Evangelical Anglicans (sometimes called "low church") place a strong emphasis on personal conversion, on preaching, on the authority of Scripture. Anglo-Catholics (sometimes called "high church") place a strong emphasis on sacramental worship, on the tradition of the church. Some hold a conservative view on issues such as the ordination of women. Other "liberal Catholics" support the ordination of women. Charismatic Anglicans focus on the gifts of the Holy Spirit and prefer a style of worship with contemporary music, clapping, and spontaneity. The majority of Canadian Anglicans would probably fit into a middle category that draws upon a number of Anglican traditions.

The 20th century was a period of theological exploration. Feminist theology, liberation theology, aboriginal spirituality, reflection on social and justice issues, the rediscovery of older Christian traditions, and the ecumenical movement all continue to enrich the life of our church.

The 21st century

The 21st century sees the church grappling with new issues and concerns. When all Canadian provinces and territories legalized marriages between persons of the same gender, many Canadian denominations came face to face with questions about human sexuality. Questions have been raised about the authority of scripture and the ways in which our Anglican family of churches makes decisions. Canada has become increasingly multicultural and multi-faith so we explore what it means to be part of the Canadian mosaic. Declining membership in rural areas requires us to examine how ministry can best be expressed where the population is small. Social issues such as poverty and injustice call for our response. A new relationship is being forged with indigenous Anglicans. A movement called "the emerging church" is found across a spectrum of denominations as Christians explore the Church's mission in a post-modern culture. Disillusioned with the institutional church, participants in this conversation look in new ways at worship and mission. You can learn more about these issues and the church's vision for the future in Chapters 18, 19, and 21.

3

What is Anglican Sunday worship?

Many who have come into the Anglican Church from other denominations have been drawn through the worship. It was the beauty and richness of the liturgy and its music that drew me as a teenager to make my home in the Anglican Church. Worship is at the heart of what it means to be Anglican. That is why the fiercest disputes are sometimes over the forms of liturgy, because we know that the liturgy shapes our lives.

Anglican worship is **"common prayer."** We use set liturgical texts and say together the same prayers each Sunday, with the authorized variation for the season and with particular intercessions or prayers for the day. To outsiders this set text may seem limiting or even boring. To Anglicans it provides the freedom to relax into the familiar text and to explore its facets week by week. A common text frees us from dependence on the personality, skills, and interests of the person leading worship. The text allows us to reflect on all the themes of the gospel in a regular sequence. Anglican worship may be plain or elaborate, but it always follows a common pattern.

Anglican worship is **biblical**. Our prayer books are full of Scripture, either passages directly quoted or scriptural phrases in the prayers. At each service, we read and reflect on God's Word in many forms.

Anglican worship is **sacramental**. We believe that God's grace is expressed to us through material things such as water, bread and wine, and anointing with oil. The Eucharist, celebrated week by week, is at the heart of the Church's worship. The other sacramental rites (such as Baptism) also mark important moments in our religious life.

Anglican worship involves **all our senses**. Our services involve colour, music, symbols, art, poetic language, sometimes the smell of flowers or incense, the taste of the bread and wine, touching hands at the passing of the Peace, changing postures as we kneel or stand. Our buildings remind us of our place in the story of the people of God.

Anglican worship involves **both clergy and lay people**. At one time, the priest conducted the whole service. The people participated by listening and by joining in the prayers. Now there are many opportunities for lay people of all ages to participate in worship – reading the Scriptures, leading the Prayers of the People, serving at the altar, helping to administer the bread and wine, leading the singing. If a priest is not present, lay people may lead Morning or Evening Prayer and preach the sermon. In this regard, worship has changed dramatically in the last 40 years.

Two books for worship

The Book of Common Prayer is part of the very beginning of the Anglican Church. First produced in 1549, it defined the character of Anglicanism. It has gone through many revisions, each new version reflecting a theological shift from earlier editions.

The first Prayer Book was in English and was actually a reworking of the old Latin services. It steered a cautious course between the Catholic and Protestant emphases. It was too conservative for European reformers. So, in 1552, the second Prayer Book moved towards a more "reformed" theology and practice. For example, it forbade wearing vestments or making the sign of the cross in baptism.

In the time of Elizabeth, the third Prayer Book (1559) returned to a more moderate course. It permitted more ornaments in churches and restored vestments for the clergy. It also restored the phrase, "The body of Christ given for you" in the Mass or Eucharist.

The fourth Prayer Book, authorized by James I in 1604, made few changes, in spite of Puritan demands. It was the first Prayer Book authorized for use by Convocation, the governing body of the English church.

The fifth Prayer Book (1662) remained the standard text until revisions in the 20th century. Authorized by an act of Parliament, it was, once again, a return to the middle way, a combining of traditions. Because it followed a period of political instability, it includes many references to the monarchy and to political order. It also instituted a rite for adult baptism, since there had been a long period with few infant baptisms. The 1662 Prayer Book was revised in 1918 and again in 1959 in Canada.

The 20th century saw a renewed interest in liturgy worldwide. One of the aims of the liturgical movement has been to restore the participation of the people in worship, and to make the Eucharist the central service of parish worship. Scholars have discovered liturgical texts of the early church and have incorporated insights from these into new books of prayer.

Anglicans all over the world have translated *The Book of Common Prayer* into the local languages and developed alternative liturgies incorporating historic and contemporary texts and allowing for more involvement of the lay people in worship. Just as *The Book of Common Prayer* links all parts of the Anglican Communion, so our contemporary texts join us in the international movement for liturgical renewal.

In Canada, *The Book of Alternative Services* was authorized in 1985 as an alternative to *The Book of Common Prayer*. It does not contain all the material in the Prayer Book and does not replace it as the official prayer book of the church. But it is an alternative in contemporary language authorized for use by General Synod and by the diocesan bishop. In 1998, the Anglican Church of Canada also published a new hymn book, *Common Praise*, that includes traditional and contemporary hymns from many traditions.

Liturgical revision is an ongoing process. Inclusive language and a wider range of images for God, our partnership with First Nations, Metis and Inuit Anglicans, and new ways of exploring faith in today's Canadian society are all issues to be explored. Our relationship of full communion with the Evangelical Lutheran Church in Canada commits us both to co-operating with each other in revising our liturgical texts.

The introduction to the *BAS* reminds us that "the Church must be open to liturgical change in order to maintain sensitivity to the impact of the gospel on the world and to permit the continuous development of a living theology" (p. 10).

Coming together as a worshipping community

We come together each week to hear and explore the Scriptures, to give thanks for God's goodness, to pray for our own needs and the needs of the world, and to celebrate the Eucharist. We worship as a community, called by God to serve the world. We come together to support and strengthen each other.

In our baptismal vows, we promise to "continue in the apostles' teaching and fellowship, in the breaking of bread, and in the prayers." Our first promise then is to join with other Christians in the worship of God.

Some people say that you can be a Christian without going to church. They claim that Christianity is simply about a personal relationship with God. But in my view, being a Christian means being part of a community of people called by God to worship and to serve. Corporate worship helps us keep our focus on the values of the gospel, and service to others keeps our worship connected to our daily living. So coming together each week for worship, study, and community is central to our lives as Christians.

The setting for worship

Most people are introduced to the Anglican Church through Sunday worship. Usually, this worship takes place in a church building, although some congregations meet in schools or community halls, or even the homes of members. There is no single style of church architecture, and decorations and customs vary.

But there are some things that all Anglican churches have in common. One is the centrality of the altar (sometimes called the Holy Table). Because the Eucharist is the central service of worship, the altar where the Eucharist is celebrated has the central position at the front of Anglican churches. The area around the altar is usually called the sanctuary. The pulpit from which the sermon is preached and the lectern from which the Scriptures are read are usually off to the side. You will seldom find an Anglican church in which the pulpit or choir are given the central place of prominence.

The other piece of furniture found in all Anglican churches is the font, where baptisms take place. Often the font is near the entrance, as a sign that baptism is the door by which we enter into membership in the church.

Hangings, banners, candles, stained glass windows, symbols, and decorations all vary. But Anglicans agree that visual symbols remind us of God's presence. So you will usually find lots of colour (according to the church season) and a variety of symbols in each church.

Though our services are set out in prayer books, it is sometimes hard to find your way around at first. And customs, gestures, and traditions vary so much from place to place that new arrivals often need to take time to get their bearings when visiting a different parish. Increasingly, there are parishes that print the text in the leaflet or project it onto a screen. This eliminates the need to search for the right page in the prayer book.

Archbishop Ted Scott, a former Primate, once said that the most important change in our church in recent years was the introduction of the coffee hour following the Sunday morning service. Certainly the gathering of the community has been greatly enriched by opportunities for parishioners to meet and talk more informally.

Varieties of Sunday services

Today in Anglican churches you are most likely to find the Eucharist being celebrated as the principal service on a Sunday morning. Alternatively, you may find the service of Morning or Evening Prayer. These services are often called the "Office," from the Latin *officium*, meaning "work" or "duty." Although most of us are familiar with them as Sunday services, they began as daily prayers.

The custom of saying daily prayers at particular hours of the day comes to us from Jewish tradition. The apostles prayed at certain hours (Acts 10:9 and 16:25) and the Christian church continued this custom, with daily morning and evening prayers in the home.

In the 4th and 5th centuries, Christians began to gather in larger churches for daily prayer. About the same time, the monastic movement began, as some Christians wished to live in a community devoted to prayer and work.

Gradually, patterns of prayer developed, and monks or nuns gathered for worship at fixed times. The daily office included Lauds, Prime, Terce, Sext, None, Vespers, and Compline, plus the early morning office of Matins (which in many monasteries was at 2:00 a.m.).

The pattern of the office was fixed by St. Benedict in the sixth century and became the norm for monastic houses in Western Christianity. The form of service became known as the Divine Office, and consisted of prayers, scripture reading, and the recitation of large sections of the Psalter (the book of Psalms). Gradually the monastic pattern became the pattern for all ordained Christians. At the same time, though, the practice of daily corporate prayer for the laity almost ceased.

Parish clergy often found it difficult to follow the monastic pattern. Those who still used the daily office tended to compress the services into two groups, morning and evening prayer. Archbishop Cranmer accepted this popular pattern and shaped the prayers into two services, Morning and Evening Prayer. The older name "Matins" was given to the morning office. (In monastic references, the word is usually spelled "Matins"; Anglican custom uses the spelling "Mattins.")

Like all the reformers, Cranmer was anxious to have more of the Bible read in daily worship and wanted it to be read continuously. By reducing the daily office to two services and translating those two services into English, the Archbishop hoped to encourage lay people as well as clergy to use this form of prayer. The saying of the daily office was made mandatory for all clergy, a pattern that continues to this day in the Anglican Church. *The Book of Common Prayer* (page lvi) says,

> *All Priests and Deacons, unless prevented by sickness or other cause, are to say daily the Morning and Evening Prayer, either privately, or openly in the Church.*

With the Reformation and the publishing of the prayers of the church in English, lay people could participate in the daily prayers of the Church. This practice continues to be encouraged as a part of Anglican spirituality. The Prayer Book direction to priests to say prayers daily also instructs clergy to ring the church bell so that lay people can join in the daily prayers in the church.

Today many Anglicans pray regularly using forms found in *The Book of Common Prayer* or *The Book of Alternative Services*, or a pocket version such as *Celebrating Common Prayer*, a daily prayer book developed by Anglican Franciscans in England. These forms of daily service include reading Scripture, reciting Psalms, and saying prayers. Anglicans follow many different patterns of private prayer.

At the time of the Reformation, the English were accustomed to **attending** Mass each Sunday but only **receiving** Communion (the consecrated bread and wine) once or twice a year. The importance of the Eucharist was understood to centre on the offering made to God, rather than on the movement of God to us in Holy Communion. Although the framers of *The Book of Common Prayer* encouraged frequent communion, the three-fold service of Morning Prayer, Litany (a set of responsive intercessions found in *The Book of Common Prayer* following Morning and Evening Prayer), and Holy Communion became the usual Sunday morning pattern.

But people were slow to change their customs and did not wish to communicate very often. Most Anglicans left the church before Holy Communion, or did not go forward to make their communion. As a result, Holy Communion remained popular only on the greater feasts. Later the Litany was dropped, hymns were added, and Morning Prayer became the principal Sunday morning service in most parish churches. Indeed, the centrality of the Eucharist as the principal act of Sunday worship only re-emerged in the 20th century.

The Offices of Morning and Evening Prayer both follow a similar pattern. At their centre is the reading of scripture from the Old and New Testaments, the use of canticles or songs from Scripture, the systematic reading of the Psalter, the affirmation of faith or creed, and prayers. These offices give us a systematic way to immerse ourselves in the scriptural stories and to learn the hymns of praise (the Psalms) that were used by Jesus himself.

Reading through the Scriptures

Anglicans follow a lectionary, or an arrangement of Bible readings, to ensure that a large portion of the Bible is read over several years. The *BCP* lectionary for Morning and Evening Prayer is set out on pages xvi to xlv. It follows a two-year pattern for Sunday readings, and a one-year pattern for daily readings. The epistles and gospels for the Eucharist are printed in full from pages 94–330.

In 1980, the Anglican Church of Canada, along with many other churches, adopted the Common Lectionary (now the *Revised Common Lectionary*), a system of Bible readings worked out by an ecumenical group of Canadian and American scholars. The Sunday lectionary (in the *BAS* pages 268–439) follows a three-year pattern and so includes more of the Scriptures. An Old Testament lesson was added to the Eucharistic readings.

The Daily Office lectionary is a two-year pattern of readings, found in the *BAS* (pages 452–497). This is the lectionary used for daily prayer. From time to time, there are revisions to these lists of readings.

Morning Prayer or Mattins

Services of Morning and Evening Prayer may be conducted by lay people.

The service may begin with penitential prayers. We confess our sins and are assured of God's forgiveness. This introduction to prayer is particularly appropriate in the seasons of Advent and Lent.

Morning worship begins with the saying of Psalm 95, called the *Venite* (from the Latin opening words of the psalm, "O come"). This is a psalm of praise to call us to worship. In the Jewish tradition, this psalm is still used at the beginning of synagogue worship.

Regular saying of the psalms is the cornerstone of the Office. At each service, one or more psalms are read, so that the whole Psalter is covered over a period of time. The psalms are the hymn book of the Jewish religion. This recitation connects us with our roots in the Hebrew tradition as well as with our own Christian history.

Lessons are read from the Old and New Testaments. The custom of reading Scripture is an important part of Anglican worship that stems from the 16th century and connects us with the Reformation.

Canticles are songs from the Bible, other than the Psalms. Some of these, like the *Gloria in Excelsis* and the *Te Deum*, are early Christian writings. Both the *BCP* and the *BAS* contain a good deal of Scripture in the canticles and prayers. We sing or recite these canticles as part of our response to the readings. The following are commonly used at Morning Prayer:

- *Te Deum Laudamus* ("We Praise Thee, O God"), a Latin hymn of the early church;
- *Benedictus* ("Blessed Be"), the Song of Zechariah, Luke 1:68–79;
- *Jubilate Deo* ("O Be Joyful in God"), Psalm 100.

The *BAS* suggests a variety of canticles on pages 72–95.

The sermon should provide a commentary on the readings. It doesn't have to be long but should help us reflect on what God is saying to us today. A sermon **must** be preached at the Eucharist but is not required at Morning or Evening Prayer.

We profess our faith in the words of the creed. The Apostles' Creed was developed by the early church as a brief way of setting out the essentials of the Christian faith. The creed's three paragraphs correspond to the three Persons of God the Trinity: God as Father, Son, and Holy Spirit. This creed is used at the baptismal service, and at Morning and Evening Prayer. The *BAS* also permits its use at the Eucharist. The Nicene Creed, a longer statement of faith deriving from the 4th and 5th centuries, is most commonly used at the Eucharist.

The *BAS* offers as an alternative "Hear O Israel" drawn from the *Shema* (Hebrew, "Hear"), the Jewish confession of faith. All Jewish men are required to recite this confession of faith every morning and evening. The words are found in Deuteronomy 6:4, 5 and Mark 12:29–31.

The service concludes with prayers, including the Lord's Prayer and the Collect of the Day. The Collect is the name given to a particular prayer for each week. It "collects" up the thoughts and prayers of all congregation members in a single prayer. Each Sunday of the year has a different collect, and there are collects for special days, such as saints days.

Evening Prayer or Evensong

Evening Prayer follows almost the same pattern, with the recitation of psalms, the reading of lessons from the Old and New Testaments, and the saying of prayers.

The canticles most commonly used at Evensong are

- the Magnificat ("magnifies") or Song of Mary, Luke 1:46–55
- the *Nunc Dimittis* ("Now You Dismiss") or Song of Simeon, Luke 2:29–32

At one time, many churches had a regular Sunday evening service. Many Anglicans remember these services as a special time of quiet prayer and reflection at the end of a busy Sunday. A few parish churches and cathedrals have maintained the tradition but it is not as widespread as it once was. There is much beautiful music written for both Mattins and Evensong, an important part of our heritage as Anglicans.

Compline is a late-evening service, a service of quiet reflection at the end of the day. It is often used at conferences and retreats as the act of worship that brings the day to a close. The service includes psalms and prayers suitable for evening.

4

What happens in church the rest of the week?

Church is more than one hour of worship on Sunday morning. Most parishes are hives of activity all week long, with organizations, study groups, and ministry to the neighbourhood. These activities may happen in the church building or in the homes of congregation members.

The central reason for our coming together is for worship. But we are also called by God to be part of a community that meets for support and friendship and fun for ourselves, and for service to others.

Anglican Church Women

One of the most popular Anglican organizations is the **Anglican Church Women**. Branches can be found in parishes in all parts of Canada.

ACW began life as a group called the **Women's Auxiliary**. In 1885, Roberta Tilton and six other women went to the House of Bishops and asked for permission to set up a national organization for women which would unite the various groups interested in mission. The bishops authorized the establishment of the "Women's Auxiliary to the Domestic and Foreign Missionary Society of the Church of England in Canada," often known as WA for short. The Winchester Cross was adopted as the badge of the organization. The WA devoted itself to a program of mission and Bible study, fundraising, and fellowship and support for its own members. WA groups raised funds by bake sales, catering, rummage sales, and teas. Often the funds raised by the women of the parish helped to furnish the church, pay the rector's salary, and sustain the parish on a sound financial footing.

During periods like the Depression of the 1930s, the contributions of the WA and other groups of women kept parishes going. During all the years when women were not part of vestries, council, and synods, their behind-the-scenes role made an important difference to the life of the church. Overseas missions were a special focus of the work of the WA. For many years, this organization supported women missionaries overseas and in the north and west of Canada.

The **Mothers' Union** was founded as a parish organization in England in 1876 by Mary Sumner. It became a diocesan organization in 1885 and came to Canada in 1888, although it is less widespread here than the ACW. Its aims are to encourage, strengthen, and support marriage and family life. Women meet for prayer and study, and to provide fellowship and support in local communities, organize development projects around the world, and lobby governments on issues involving family life. MU is found worldwide; in fact, it is the largest international women's organization in the church. Archbishop Rowan Williams, in an address to the World Council of Churches meeting in Brazil, described it as "the most powerful lay movement in the Anglican world."

A parish may also have a Guild or a Circle or other group of women who meet regularly outside of the national organizations to study and to raise funds to assist the work of the congregation.

In 1966, it was decided to integrate the work of various women's organizations. The WA was disbanded and reformed as Anglican Church Women. Its missionary work became integrated with the World Mission program of the national church. ACW was originally designed as an umbrella organization that would include all women, both those who belong to formal groups and those who do not. It was hoped that the change would involve more women in church matters, would free women from the burden of fundraising, and would enable men and women to work more closely together in the church. Some dioceses had integrated Councils that included former WA members, Mothers' Union members and women not members of guilds or groups. The hope was then and is now that all Anglican women will consider themselves to be part of ACW.

Some of the earlier organization has persisted. Many dioceses charge membership fees and make annual contributions to the diocese and the national church. Each year, diocesan Presidents of ACW and their counterparts who chair diocesan committees for women's concerns meet to share ideas and resources and study how to respond to the needs and concerns of women in the church. Today the ACW is a loosely knit fellowship of women whose purpose is to give women the opportunity "to unite in a fellowship of worship, study, and service which will lead them into Christian service in the parish, community, diocese, nation and the world." The National ACW Executive provides a national forum and voice for women in the Anglican Church of Canada.

Today's dilemma

At one time, most women in a parish belonged to the women's group. Now times have changed. Membership has declined. Active members are getting older and less able to do fundraising and catering. Most younger women work outside the home. Their lives are hectic, with job, family, and community responsibilities. They are reluctant to commit themselves to meeting once a month, though they may be willing to help out from time to time. In a time when family life is fragmented, family members may choose to spend together what free time they have.

This dilemma is true not just for Anglican organizations, or even just church groups. Many service clubs, volunteer organizations, and community groups also face the problems of declining membership and the increasing age of volunteers.

This time of change is a difficult one for members. Most have been part of close-knit groups whose members shared each other's joys and sorrows over a lifetime. Perhaps they joined the same group while they were young married women, raised their children, shared the joys and sorrows of everyday life, had the fun of working and studying together, and now are in their senior years with less energy to work in the kitchen but with a deep appreciation for the Christian companionship and support of the group. To some, it seems as though something precious is being cast aside, not valued.

I hope that, as a church, we find new ways for all of us to study, work, and pray together – in women's and men's groups, in mixed and family groups, in parish get-togethers and events. I hope that we can all celebrate the past and look with hope and enthusiasm to new ways of responding to the mission of the church.

Men's groups

The **Brotherhood of Anglican Churchmen** is an organization of Anglican men "to back the church more effectively by being living examples of their belief in the faith." It was formed in the Diocese of Huron in 1951. Members meet in parish groups for study, prayer, and service. They pledge themselves to regular church attendance and active participation in parish life and in outreach to the wider community. Groups are found in a number of dioceses across the country.

There are also many other men's groups that meet in parishes for study and fellowship, and to carry out parish and community projects.

Children

At one time, there were a great many church groups for children and young people. The Women's Auxiliary sponsored a number of groups. Little Helpers was an opportunity to support in prayer the families of newly baptized children. Cards were sent and gatherings of mothers and children held. In the 1960s the focus of Little Helpers changed to an emphasis on family life and the teaching of family life skills in workshops and study programs. Some ACWs still maintain a Little Helpers program today.

The WA also had programs for girls: the Junior Auxiliary for younger girls, and the Girls' Auxiliary for teenagers. Girls wore uniforms, earned badges, studied the Christian faith, and had lots of fun at meetings. A few dioceses today have groups of juniors that preserve some of the traditions. Often these groups are open to both boys and girls.

Organizations for boys included the Boys' Brigade and the Church Boys' League. Again, some of these groups continue in parts of the country.

Churches have always been supportive of the Scouting movement, and many Scouting organizations have met in Anglican church halls. These have been an important part of church life. These organizations offer a Religion and Life badge which can be an occasion for Christian education programming in the parish.

There are often other less formal midweek groups for children the Wednesday Club, Kids' Club, midweek church school, recreation programs, or drop-in care. Children are members of the church because they are baptized, and parish halls are great places for them to meet, learn, and have fun. Messy Church is a program for families – a "once a month time of creativity, worship, and eating together" where parents and children can gather for a couple of hours in a relaxed atmosphere.

Secular organizations

There are many other community groups that meet in Anglican churches: Alcoholics Anonymous and similar self-help organizations, day care and pre-school associations, cultural and recreational groups, social service projects of outreach to the community such as food banks, breakfast or lunch programs, clothing depots, and thrift shops.

Young adults

The Anglican Young People's Association was a lively organization in our church in the '50s and '60s. Many of today's church leaders became active in the church through the AYPA. The Anglican Youth Movement was active in many parishes and dioceses in the 1980s and 1990s. (The AYM is still very active in one part of the country – the British Columbia/ Yukon AYM or BCYAYM.) Today the national church employs a part-time consultant on youth work and many dioceses employ diocesan coordinators to help parishes plan for the needs and concerns of teenagers. Young people have opportunities to participate in all aspects of the church's mission and ministry: outreach, music, faith formation, visioning, and governance, including serving as a youth synod delegate. Many dioceses have youth synods or annual youth conferences where they explore issues, grow in faith, and articulate their vision of the church.

Since 2007, the Youth Initiatives Working Group has identified and monitored youth ministries across Canada in order to support this work. Ask and Imagine, held each summer since 1999 at Huron College, is a residential program for high school students and young adults that engages them in exploring theology, and ministry and leadership skills. Justice Camps, for young and older adults learning together, and developed by the Ecojustice Committee and Partners in Mission, have been held annually in various parts of Canada since 2005. Since 2010, Anglicans and Lutherans have participated in bi-annual national youth gatherings (Canadian Lutheran Anglican Youth or CLAY), building on our relationship of full communion. National gatherings have been held for youth leaders for training and building networks. Further information can be found at the website of the Anglican Church of Canada and a website for youth ministry concerns, www.generation.anglican.ca.

Like the children, adolescents are not just the "future members" of the church but are present members and should be deeply involved in the life and work of the Anglican Church.

Christian education

Today there is an emphasis on the education of the laity, and a new hunger for serious study. Adults are meeting in groups to study the Bible, Church history, current issues, and skills for living the Christian life. Parish groups, regional or diocesan events, and national gatherings all offer excellent opportunities for study. Seminaries and theological colleges, lay training centres, and schools of theology offer courses for interested lay people as well as clergy.

Education for Ministry is an extension program of the University of the South in Sewanee, Tennessee, that offers a four-year program of theological and biblical study for lay people. Small groups meet weekly with a trained mentor to discuss what they have been reading and to engage in theological reflection on events of daily life. This program is found in many dioceses of our church.

Cursillo (Spanish for "little course") is a weekend format with instruction in the faith, time for worship, and an opportunity to build community. "Cursillistas" – people who have attended a cursillo weekend – are encouraged to meet regularly for continuing nurture and spiritual growth.

And there are many, many other groups within dioceses and parishes: Bible study groups, Marriage Encounter (a weekend opportunity for couples to strengthen their marriages), the Order of St. Luke that meets to pray and promote healing, renewal groups, book groups, groups that meet for prayer and praise or to discuss particular social issues, groups that sponsor refugees, feminist discussion groups, support groups for people with particular needs...

We are becoming a "learning" church. I think it is great to see the interest in and enthusiasm for study. I see it strengthening our church, and in ways we cannot imagine!

The education of children

These days, in many Anglican churches, children may meet with their teachers for religious instruction during part of the Sunday morning service. In other churches, children and adults meet jointly or separately for learning at times other than the service. During classes, children and adults worship together, explore the Bible and Christian faith, use art, music, or drama to reflect on what they have learned, play games, and build a sense of community.

There is a variety of resource material available for children and young adults. Many churches use curriculum materials based on the lectionary. Everyone in the church reads the same biblical material and reflects on it as appropriate to their age and ability. Other parishes use theme-based curriculum materials. Music, drama, crafts, and storytelling bring a rich experience to the exploration of the Christian faith.

5

How do I live a Christian life every day?

Anglicans believe that God is involved in the stuff of everyday life. So we see our daily life and work in terms of ministry. Being Christian is not just a Sunday occupation. Our faith influences our whole life. What we do Monday to Saturday is related to our Sunday mornings. Our worship should inform every aspect of our life: our work, our leisure, our relationships.

Some writers use the terms "Saturday, Sunday, and Monday" ministries as ways to describe different aspects of our Christian witness. Let's look first at our Sunday ministries, as it is easiest for most people to see ministry as what we do at the church on Sundays.

Sunday ministries

Fifty years ago it was common for clergy to function in the parish as the "one man band." (In those days, the clergy **were** all men, so this is not a sexist remark!) The priest was in charge of the parish. He made most of the decisions, chaired most of the meetings, took all the Sunday and midweek services, did all the visiting. The priest took all parts of the Sunday service himself; read the lessons, spoke the prayers, preached the sermon, and celebrated the Eucharist. Lay people formed the choir and took up the collection but apart from that simply sat in the pews and followed along in the Prayer Book.

Recently however, the Anglican Church has come to a new understanding of the meaning of Baptism. Baptism means we become full members of the family of the Church with privileges and responsibilities. We are all called to ministry at all times.

Verna Dozier, an Episcopalian laywoman and educator, wrote in *The Authority of the Laity* (p. 3),

In the clerical mind, "lay ministry" ranges all the way from "finding something for the lay people to do" to "getting some help with the work because I can't do it all." In the minds of most laity, "lay ministry" means being let in on the institution's work – or being trapped into it.

As laity, we come to church on Sundays to worship God, to learn, to be fed, and to be strengthened by God in the gathered community. Lay people also take part in worship and hospitality. Here are some of the lay ministries that you may see. (All ministries are open to women and men.)

- **Greeters** welcome you to the parish, give you a leaflet, and introduce you to some members if you are new to the parish.
- **Readers** read the lessons from Scripture and lead the congregation in the reading of the psalm.
- **Intercessors** lead the prayers of the people, gathering up the concerns of individuals, of the parish, of the diocese and the wider church, of the secular community.
- **Sidespeople** take up the collection or offering and present it at the altar. Sometimes members from a parish family will bring up the bread and wine from the back of the church.
- **Servers or Acolytes** assist during the celebration of the Eucharist. They light candles, assist the priest in preparing the altar for communion and in cleaning up, and do whatever other jobs are asked of them. A server who carries the processional cross is sometimes called a **crucifer**. Where incense is used, the server who carries the thurible or incense burner is called a **thurifer** and the incense is carried in a small "boat" by a "boat boy" or "boat girl"!
- **Choir members** or choristers, adults and children, lead the music for worship. Many parts of the Anglican service can be sung, so the choir may be kept very busy in some parishes. Choirs lead in the music of hymns, canticles, psalms, parts of the Eucharistic prayer like the

Sanctus, the Lord's Prayer and other prayers. In addition, choirs may sing an anthem during the service. Churches without choirs still can have lots of music in the service with congregational singing. Anglicans use many different styles of music that may be accompanied by guitars, flutes, trumpets, or recorders as well as organs and pianos.

• **Communion assistants** go by many different titles. These lay people are authorized by the bishop to assist in the distribution of the bread and wine at communion.

• **Church school teachers** have an important ministry in the Christian education of children, young people, and adults. Often they must be absent from church themselves so that they can teach their classes. Sometimes parish education happens at other times, such as before the Sunday service or during the week. **Nursery helpers** look after the babies.

• **Churchwardens** (along with the rector) are signing officers for the parish and are responsible to the bishop for its administration. There must be at least two wardens, one elected by the people and often called the People's Warden, and one appointed by the priest or minister (Rector or Incumbent) called the Rector's Warden.

• **Vestry** or **Parish Council** members are elected by parishioners to administer the affairs of the parish. The parish elects **synod delegates** to represent the parish in the decisions of Diocesan Synod. The canons or rules of the diocese specify how all these offices work.

• **Children and youth** need to share in ministry during the worship service and in parish life. Children and teenagers are not "future members" of the church. They are present members by virtue of their baptism, and they need to be offered responsibilities suitable to their age and ability They can read lessons, lead prayers, sing, play musical instruments, serve at the altar, bring forward the offering, and help administer the communion.

Unfortunately, we have not always welcomed the young to our Sunday ministries. We are gradually learning what it means to be a family of many generations, each person called by God to ministry within the church and the world.

Monday ministries

Our Monday ministry takes place where we live and work, where we go to school, within the political, environmental, economic, and social systems that we are a part of. How do I live responsibly as Christian where I work? In my school? While I shop?

What we do in church on Sunday ought to prepare us for what happens to us during the rest of the week. So we look to the church community for guidance and help in the difficult decisions we have to make, in the discouragement and triumphs of our weekday life. We are strengthened by worship and fed by the sacraments. And we also need help reflecting on ethical dilemmas, the challenges of life in our community, the demands of our job.

I once taught in an elementary school where I felt that the staff room had been poisoned by the foul language and dirty jokes of some of the staff. I was only a temporary substitute but if I had been on permanent staff I would have had to decide what to do about it. What response should I make, as a Christian? How could I make a difference, in a way that would be helpful rather than simply judgmental? I wish I had been able to talk with others about the situation.

And how do we support people whose jobs require them to act against their conscience? Business firms demand that their employees be competitive, and concerned only with making a profit for the company. Sometimes this creates a dilemma for those employees when they see company policy conflict with issues of compassion and justice.

- How does a Christian stockbroker, for example, handle currency trading in difficult economic times, when his actions may benefit his client, but hurt his country?
- What are the ethical dilemmas for those in today's health care system? Health care personnel face difficult decisions with issues such as participating in procedures that prolong or end life, overcrowding, and understaffing.
- How do we support those whose jobs are boring and demeaning? Many jobs today are repetitive, such as entering data into computers or working on an assembly line. How does one find meaning or value in such repetition?

- Work in certain kinds of jobs, such as the tobacco or armaments industries, may provide financial security, but may raise ethical questions about the end product of the work.
- Anglicans have always been involved in the political process, in civic, provincial and federal government. How does their membership in the church illuminate their work in the political process? Does it make a difference?
- How should a Christian student respond to peer pressure, bullying, sexism, violence in the schools, unemployment, or rising tuition fees?
- Many middle-aged middle-management people are losing their jobs, at a time in life when they expected that their security would be well established. Many of them are church members. Many of those who have to enforce the staff cuts are also parishioners, and face great pain in this demand of their job. So an Anglican bank manager must foreclose on the farm of a fellow parishioner. And the parish must respond to the needs and concerns of both.
- How do we balance our environmentally damaging behaviours with the needs of the environment? How does our work and play affect all others in creation?

I think that we need to help people talk about their stressors. Our churches should provide a place where Anglicans can meet together to share their deepest concerns. Groups of teachers or forest workers or farmers or bankers need to reflect on what "Monday ministry" means in their place of work. A Monday morning breakfast group where parishioners meet before work, a workplace group of Christians in an office, a gathering of teachers or those in similar occupations are just a few examples of opportunities for reflection on ministry in daily life and work. We believe in a good God, who created all the world, who redeems and strengthens us, and is involved in our everyday lives.

One excellent resource is *The Monday Connection: On Being an Authentic Christian in a Weekday World,* by William E. Diehl (HarperCollins, 1993). The author, for many years manager of sales at Bethlehem Steel, has written a fine book for lay people to help us make connections between what we do in church and what we do in the workplace. The Anglican Church of Canada website lists many resources for baptismal ministry formation. See the Episcopal Church (United States) and Evangelical Lutheran Church in America websites: www.episcopalchurch.org/mdl.htm and www.elca.org/dailylifeministry.

We express our beliefs about God in the way we act at home, in business, on the golf course. As church members, we need to understand how God is present to us in everyday life, how we can make responsible Christian decisions in our complex world. Lisa Chisholm-Smith writes on the Diocese of Ottawa website that God cares deeply for weekday worlds – the places where we live, learn, work, play, and volunteer – and for the people who share these places with us. God chooses to use us in those very places as agents for Christ's kingdom.

We need to hold in our intercessions people in all kinds of work situations – those who must make difficult decisions, those whose jobs bring them little meaning or satisfaction, those who face unemployment. What is the Good News of the gospel for them?

We need to celebrate all the saints, all the baptized who are striving to follow Jesus Christ in every part of their lives – for garage mechanics who keep our cars running, for child care workers who care for our children, for cleaners who look after offices and homes, for artists and writers and musicians, for medical personnel and supermarket cashiers. All of these are Christian vocations, and part of our job is to follow Jesus "into every walk of life," as this Canadian prayer tells us.

Draw your Church together, O Lord,
into one great company of disciples,
together following our Lord Jesus Christ
into every walk of life,
together serving him in his mission to the world,
and together witnessing to his love
on every continent and island. (BAS, p. 676)

Saturday ministries

For me, Saturday represents leisure time, families, hobbies and sports, and the cultural life of our community.

Part of our Saturday ministry is to care for ourselves. Many churches are finding that a lot of volunteers are burning out. They began as willing helpers and then find themselves swamped by demands of parish, home, and community. As children of God, we need to care for ourselves, to rest and be refreshed, to allow ourselves to spend quiet time recharging our batteries. So sometimes our Saturday ministry means saying no to requests for more volunteer hours.

As part of our response to the gospel, we need to spend time with our families, caring for and supporting them. Saturday ministry reminds us that taking time for our family is a ministry too.

In this chapter, you will see that I have devoted a number of pages to Sunday ministries, a smaller number to Monday ministries, and only a few paragraphs to Saturday ministries. That is, I suspect, a fairly accurate representation of how much we think of our activities on those days as ministries. It is hard for us to think of our leisure time, our family life, as ministries in the same way as the more public areas of our lives. As church members, we need to identify and celebrate our Saturday ministries too.

Our leisure activities, our travel, our shopping, our games and hobbies are all areas where we try to live out the meaning of our Christian vocation. God gives us many great opportunities and gifts in our Saturdays, as well as our Sundays and Mondays. How do we use these gifts of God?

6

What is stewardship?

When we talk about stewardship in church, people often assume that this is just another conversation about money. How can the parish get more money? How can it spend less? How can it balance its budget?

But stewardship is really more about theology and our response to God's gifts. Stewardship explores what it means to be created by God and placed in the world God has made, with the other people whom God has made.

All our reflection on money and possessions, on the earth as our home, begins with the amazing generosity of God. God created the world and all that is in it. God created human beings, gave all creatures the gift of life, and sustains that life every day. We have been given great gifts and talents. So the first part of stewardship is giving thanks to God for all the good things that we have received.

We speak about this gratitude in our prayer, "All things come of thee, and of thine own have we given thee." (*BCP*, p. 74) All good gifts come from God, and it is God's own gifts to us that we return with thanks and praise. We give our money, our time, and our talents because God has first given to us.

At the same time, we live in community – the community of all human beings, first of all, and then the smaller communities of town, church, workplace, and family. We also live in the earth community. We are closely connected to other people, all beings, and earth's natural systems; none of us lives a completely solitary life. We are bound together, affected by the joys and sorrows and actions of others, and the health of the earth. We are interdependent; we need the gifts others have to share. And others need our gifts of time, resources, and wise and loving actions. The Christian church recognizes the need to care for others, and for the earth. So stewardship has something to do with money. But it has much more to do with discipleship. We give because Jesus calls us to share, care for, and support others, and to live with respect in creation.

The baptismal covenant (*BAS*, p. 159) reminds us that we are to "proclaim by word and example the good news of God in Christ," to "seek and serve Christ in all persons," and to "strive for justice and peace among all people." By our baptism, we are called to bring good news to all and work to ensure that all people enjoy the quality of life that God intends for them. "Salvation" comes from a Hebrew word which has at its root the idea of "room to live." We need to build a society where people have room to grow and to flourish, to become the people God intends them to be. Our gifts are to be shared to help to bring this about.

When we give generously of our time and gifts and money, we may find that we receive back more than we give – the joy of sharing with others, the satisfaction of contributing to the building up of society, the expanding of our community to include other people. Our lives are enriched as we look outside our immediate circle to the wider world. John Bunyan, author of *Pilgrim's Progress,* wrote in the 17th century, "A man there was, though some did count him mad, the more he cast away, the more he had."

Our money

Although stewardship is about more than money, it certainly includes making decisions about the money we have. We live in a material world. We need houses and food and clothing. We receive wages and payment for the work we do. As a society, we share our resources to provide health care and schools and highways. The church, as institution, must also be concerned with money in order to accomplish the mission to which God is calling us.

Jesus spoke frequently about money. He spoke about selling everything and giving to the poor (Mark 10:21), about how hard it is for people burdened by possessions to enter the kingdom of heaven (Matthew 19:23), about using wealth to buy the one treasure of great value (Matthew 13:45). He became angry at the tax collectors who stole from the poor (Luke 19:45–46) and praised the widow who gave as her offering everything that she had (Mark 12:41–44). Many of his parables are concerned with landowners, wealthy merchants, coins lost and found, talents saved and spent. He seems to have acknowledged the need to pay taxes, to "render to Caesar," and the need to care for the disadvantaged of society.

It is right for us to be concerned about money. *The Book of Common Prayer* reminds us,

It is the duty of every parishioner to contribute regularly of his substance, as God shall prosper him, to the maintenance of the worship of God and the spread of the Gospel. (p. 66)

How money is used in the parish

The money given to the church each week is used both in the local setting and in the wider church. In the parish, the money we contribute pays the salaries of clergy, lay employees, the secretary, the verger or caretaker, the organist, and the choir director.

My mother, a lifelong church member, was astonished to discover that the priest's salary came from money placed on the collection plate. She had always assumed that salaries were paid from some central office and that her money went for extras, special projects, or missions. In fact, Anglican clergy are paid by money contributed by parishioners. In some cases, the diocese is able to supplement this amount. But most Anglican dioceses today no longer have extra money to subsidize parish salaries. If there is not enough money to pay clergy salaries and benefits, then ministry must be provided for in some other way.

Money from the offering pays for the upkeep of the church building – cleaning, light, heat, water, repairs to the roof. It pays for program expenses – for church school and adult education materials, for choir music and kitchen supplies. We all share in the financial decisions of the parish through our participation in the parish's annual meeting and through our elected representative on the vestry or parish council.

Some of the money goes to the diocese. Each parish is assessed an amount which represents its fair share of the diocesan work – the ministry of the bishop and other diocesan officials, hospital and other chaplaincies, education and other program work, mission and ministry in the diocese.

Some of the money goes to provincial synod for its work.

Each diocese is also asked to contribute its share to the work of the national church. This includes the ministry of the Primate and the national staff, overseas partnerships and relief and development work, work in the north and other isolated areas of Canada, national programs, communication through newspapers, videos and other media, our church's witness in the wider Canadian context through coalitions for social justice, and our membership in the Canadian Council of Churches.

Finally, as a national church, we pay our share for the work of the Anglican Communion and the World Council of Churches. These organizations link us with other parts of the Christian family, and enable us to share in the worldwide mission of the church.

How much should I give?

What you give to your parish depends on many factors – family income and expenses, special needs in the family, commitment to other charitable organizations.

Some Christians commit to "tithing," giving 10% of their income to the work of the church. Tithing is a biblical idea. In the Old Testament, people gave a tenth of their harvest to God as a sign of thanksgiving.

Some Christians give what has been called the modern tithe, 5% of income. This lower percentage recognizes that much of the social service ministry once supported through the tithe is now provided through our taxes and through donations to other community organizations. Other Christians begin with a smaller gift but set themselves a goal of where they would like to be in ten years' time, and so begin to work towards a target amount. Laurel Ayerst of St. Patrick's Church in Hudson Bay, Saskatchewan, describes her decision.

> *For many years I was afraid to make a financial commitment to God. If I gave to God, I would never be able to meet my other*

financial obligations – and these other obligations came first! I did
not trust that, if I gave to God more than I thought I could afford,
God would ensure that I had enough to meet my needs. A "leap of
faith" was required. I trusted in God, and God did not let me down.
I encourage you to take that leap of faith.

Pledging is a system of planned giving that many Anglicans like to follow. At the beginning of each year, church members indicate in writing an amount they will give each week. This helps the wardens and vestry or parish council know how much money the parish will have to work with during the year so they can prepare a budget and decide what activities and staff the parish can afford. A pledge is a promise to pay, but sometimes the unexpected happens and our circumstances change. If our plans change, and we need to adjust our giving, letting the parish officers know gives them a clear understanding of the finances available.

Most Anglican churches use a system of offering envelopes to encourage regular giving. The envelope also guarantees privacy in giving; only the financial officials of the parish know the amount of your gift. Today many church members meet their obligations through automatic debit.

Of time and talents

Money is only one of the gifts we may have. God has given each of us wonderful gifts of personality and skill – gifts of speaking and listening, of teaching and learning, of visiting and cooking and organizing.

Every congregation has members with the talents it needs to minister in the community. Stewardship means identifying and developing our own talents, and recognizing and affirming the talents of others, so that we may all respond to God's call in this community. At one time we were inclined to let the priest do the entire ministry on our behalf. Now we celebrate that each of us has the skills to build God's church here.

For example, I use my gifts and skills in teaching to do different kinds of educational work in the church. I write curriculum and other material, and lead training events and workshops. I enjoy committee work – yes, I really do! – and use that gift on national and diocesan committees. And I love to sing, so, when I get a chance, I share that gift through my church choir. I don't have much time to bake, and I've never been able to sew anything more complicated than replacing a button, so I am always grateful that there are others who have those gifts to share with me!

Some of us share our time and talents in energetic and public ways. Some of us are not able to be involved actively in the life of the congregation. But our time and talent for prayer, listening, or encouragement can be every bit as important in helping others to grow in the faith.

The life of the church depends upon its lay volunteers. Stewardship of time means that we are called to devote some of our time to building up the life of the Body of Christ. We are called to worship, study, and strengthen the Christian community. But we are also called to take care of ourselves, to allow ourselves time for rest and refreshment in the middle of the busyness of life. Sometimes church volunteers become "weary in well-doing"; the willing volunteer often finds more and more to do. Burnout is always a danger in volunteer organizations, and the church is no exception. Remember that no is also an answer. Stewardship of our time means allowing ourselves time to learn, to think, to pray, and to dream.

Stewardship education is an important part of the parish program. Church members need to explore what the gospel means in their daily lives – how following Jesus affects decisions about money, time, and talents. Many parishes have an annual stewardship visitation, when lay volunteers try to visit every family, let them know about the church and its programs, and help them to look at what this might mean in terms of family decisions. The visitation is not just about money; it is about welcoming members and helping them to feel a part of this community. Financial campaigns seem to work best when people have time to explore the issues and consider what the gospel is saying, when people are encouraged to think not merely of how large a cheque to write but of how their own talents can contribute to the strengthening of the parish family.

Children and stewardship

By their baptism, children are full members of the Body of Christ. They are members right now! Children and adolescents have great gifts to share – joy and wonder, trust and love, energy and enthusiasm, curiosity and questioning.

How can we encourage children to grow as responsible stewards of God's good gifts? David Jones and Catrina Tapley, of All Saints Westboro in Ottawa, tell their family's story.

We have an "all in" family approach to stewardship at church. Our two sons (ages seven and 14) understand that they can make a contribution to the life of the church and more broadly to society. We all volunteer in some capacity and we talk about how this makes a difference. Some contributions are a little different, such as donating to the church a portion of the sales from an art show (one of us is a professional artist) or collecting spare pennies for Granaid, a project to help AIDS orphans in South Africa. This is a really tangible way for the seven-year-old to help. More importantly for our kids, there are things that do not have a monetary focus but are equally important for the life of the church, such as being a server, helping with our church's monthly Jazz Vespers, and helping to shop for and package fresh vegetables for the parish food bank. We find that these things really help to increase our boys' sense of community and belonging.

As for our monetary contributions, with the use of direct deposit, it is easy for this to be silent or unknown in our house. Our goal is to talk openly about our monetary contributions and the need to increase these on a regular basis. When we were children, there was a weekly discussion between our parents about how much money went in each window of the church envelope. Today we show up at church, walk past the collection plate (it is not passed in our church), and don't really say much about money. (We are Anglicans, after all.) Talking to our boys about the vestry

meeting and parish funding decisions, such as a new roof, adds
some reality to what we do and why we do it.

We can help children to feel a part of the family of God by welcoming
them and the gifts they bring. We can help children express thanksgiving
for God's great gifts by encouraging them to take their part regularly in our
corporate acts of praise and thanksgiving.

Together with our children we can develop habits of caring and sharing
that form our understanding of what it means to be God's people. We learn
to share by responding to opportunities for sharing. We learn to cooperate
by working together with people of all ages. We learn to care for the
environment by cleaning up where we live.

Stewardship of the environment

The *Oxford English Dictionary* lists the word steward as most likely a
derivation of the Anglo-Saxon *stigweard* meaning "keeper of the house."
This makes it a particularly good word to use when we talk about our
responsibility for the planet on which we live. How do we care for this
earth, our home? How do we care for others, to ensure that they too have
food and shelter and all the means to grow to their full potential as children
of God? Our theology of creation reminds us that the earth is our home and
that we are entrusted with the responsibility to care for it. So concern for
environmental issues is an important part of our responsibility as Christians.
The General Synod in 2010 called upon Anglican parishes to develop
"green plans" toward making their buildings more energy efficient and to
encourage members to pursue more eco-sustainable lifestyles. There are
liturgical materials to celebrate Earth Day, the Sunday nearest April 22.

Stewardship means learning to live as members of God's family. God
created the world to be a place of justice and peace for all. All that we have
comes from God. God calls us to use our gifts to bring this vision of justice
and peace to fruition. The website of the Anglican Church of Canada has
good information about the many aspects of stewardship.

7

Is there an Anglican theology?

Some years ago, when I was describing this book to a friend, she said, "Well, **is** there a distinctive Anglican theology? I don't see how there can be. It's all Christian theology, isn't it?"

I believe that there **is** a distinctively Anglican way of doing theology, one which is quite different from other traditions. And this way of understanding theology is important for all Anglicans, lay and clergy both. When I teach, I try to demystify theology, to remove it from the box where some may try to put it. "I don't know anything about theology," a lay person may say. "I leave that to the clergy or the theologians."

But theology simply means "the word about God," and through our daily words and thoughts and actions we describe who God is for us and how we experience God. Theology deeply affects each of us. I believe that it is far too important to be left to the clergy or the professional theologians. I've read that Erasmus, a Reformation scholar and translator of the New Testament, wrote, "All can be Christians, all can be devout, and I shall boldly add – all can be theologians." We need to reclaim the study of theology for ourselves, and invite the clergy as teachers of theology to help us in this exploration.

Anglicans believe in the Incarnation, that God is present and active in the world at all times. Anglican theology is "embodied" – in liturgy, symbols, and actions – in the corporate life of the church. In worship, our theology is given practical expression, and worship is something in which both lay and clergy are involved.

Urban Holmes, in *What is Anglicanism?* defines Anglicanism as "a unique way of looking, making sense, and acting in the experience of God disclosed to us in the person of Jesus Christ," and "a manner of being conscious." (pp. 1, 2)

Anglicanism is a particular set of lenses through which we look at the revelation of God in Jesus Christ. To some extent, we do this through the lens of our history, coming from the Celtic and Roman churches of the British Isles, through the period when the British church separated itself from the power of the papacy, and continuing through the centuries of our story. We do not have one great figure, like Luther or Calvin or Wesley, to whom we point. Our history unfolds in a series of stories of faithful Christians whose responses to God at a particular time continue to instruct us today.

We are not a "confessional" church. Anglicans do not have a clearly set out document like the Augsburg Confession (Lutheran) or the Westminster Confession (Presbyterian) to which we turn for theological direction. The Thirty-Nine Articles, which came out of the theological controversies of the 16th century, have never had that force and in fact do not cover all the topics that one would want to include in a "confession of faith."

Nor have we been very good at setting out a systematic exposition of Anglican doctrine. Our style of theological discourse reflects our acceptance of the world as a place of ambiguity, a place for ongoing exploration of what the faith means when lived in such a world. As John Westerhoff, an Anglican priest and educator, writes in the foreword to his wife Caroline's book *Calling*,

> *While never anti-intellectual, Anglicans are more at home with the intuitive way of thinking and knowing than the intellectual. They prefer art to philosophy and are more comfortable in the world of symbol, myth and ritual than that of systematic theology. They are more at home with liturgy that makes use of the arts rather than discursive prose, because Anglicans affirm the anagogical, the metaphorical, the paradoxical, and the symbolic in the exploration of human experience. That is why some of their best theologians have been poets.* (pp. ix–x)

Urban Holmes says much the same thing in *What is Anglicanism?*

> *We Anglicans are not given to writing great theology. There are notable exceptions, but they are difficult to remember; but when*

Anglicanism is at its best its liturgy, its poetry, its music and its life can create a world of wonder in which it is very easy to fall in love with God. (p. 5)

Among the great Anglican writers who shape and are shaped by our distinctive way of doing theology are people like George Herbert, C. S. Lewis, William Shakespeare, T. S. Eliot, Madeleine L'Engle, and P. D. James. Poetry, fiction, drama, the literature of the imagination come easily to Anglicans. Nourished by the language of *The Book of Common Prayer*, we recognize that words are enormously important, not to be trivialized or proclaimed lightly. Words have the power to create new experience in us, and to deepen the experience of God in us.

Stephen Sykes, former Bishop of Ely and author of *Incarnation and Myth*, defined "liturgy" as "the matrix in which Anglicans are taught the Christian faith." We do not have a lot of systematic exposition of doctrine. There is no particular place where all that Anglicans believe on a particular topic is written down. Many Anglicans write on many topics, but their works are explorations rather than definitive statements required to be believed by all. What we do have are books of common prayer, which are authorized liturgical texts. In these prayer books, we learn something of what Anglicans believe. For instance, we learn what we believe about baptism by reading the words of the baptismal service. We know that the doctrine of the Incarnation is important to Anglicans because, each time we celebrate the Eucharist, we tell again the story that God entered human history, lived, suffered, and died as one of us and, by that death and resurrection, delivers us from sin and death.

Anglicans have felt a need **not** to try to define doctrine too closely. Our theologians have tried to enunciate a few essential theological principles, leaving us room to explore and expand these in our time and circumstances. The Doctrine Commission of the Church of England in its 1981 report, *Believing in the Church* said,

Statements of doctrine, then, must be provisional, tentative and infrequent. Corporate believing cannot flourish when subjected

to a mass of authoritative definitions... we define doctrine only when necessary, and the necessity is produced only by the need for immediate practical decisions. (pp. 290–291)

Examples of the need for "immediate practical decisions" were the issues of the ordination of women and the remarriage of divorced persons.

In 1987, a set of "Pastoral Guidelines for Interchurch Marriages" was agreed upon by Anglican and Roman Catholics in Canada. The introduction to those guidelines helps us to understand the different approaches to law in the two denominations. In Roman Catholic canon law, the laws are strictly stated and are to be interpreted "with all the personal adaptations contained..." In other words, there is the possibility of a number of exceptions to the laws. Anglican canon law is based on English common law. The laws are few, but are to be strictly interpreted. This is a fundamental difference: whether to define everything, including exceptions, or whether to define very little, except for the affirmation of certain fundamental principles.

Anglicans have sometimes been accused of being "wishy-washy" on doctrine, since it is hard for us to point to any particular statement of belief. I think this accusation is unfair, but it illustrates fundamental differences in approach between churches I believe that is why, in recent years, ecumenism has focused more on dialogue and on cooperation rather than on the merger of traditions. Denominations do approach the Christian faith differently.

Here are some things that make us distinctively Anglican.

Scripture, Tradition, and Reason

Anglican theology is based on three principles – Scripture, tradition, and reason. In the 16th century, the Puritans proclaimed Scripture as the supreme authority. Richard Hooker answered in *The Laws of Ecclesiastical Polity* that Scripture must always be read in the light of tradition and reason.

Scripture

A complete Bible was published in English in 1535, making the scriptures accessible for public and private reading. Archbishop Cranmer, in framing *The Book of Common Prayer*, used enormous amounts of Scripture in the canticles and prayers, in the recitation of the Psalms, and in the regular pattern of readings from the Old and New Testaments.

Article VI of the Thirty-Nine Articles declares that

Holy Scripture containeth all things necessary to salvation: so that whatsoever is not read therein, nor may be proved thereby, is not to be required of any man, that it should be believed as an article of the Faith, or be thought requisite or necessary to salvation. (BCP, p. 700)

Holy Scripture is therefore a basic authority for Anglicans.

Tradition

Tradition is the collective wisdom of the church, what the church has received and taught through the centuries. We recognize that Scripture and tradition go hand in hand.

The Bible comes to us through the church. It was the people of God who determined the canon of Scripture, which books should be included out of all the many that have been written. It is the church that interprets Scripture.

The books of the Bible come to us out of the lives of particular faith communities. Our own faith community connects our story with the story of the Bible. We learn in community and we pray in community, using the Scriptures to shape our life in the church. The church explores the teaching of Scripture as it defines doctrine, and uses Scripture to correct and reform doctrine.

The historic creeds of the church (the Nicene and Apostles' Creeds) are ways in which the early church stated its understanding of the Christian faith. Some of its definitions are based on the biblical narrative. Others – like the definition of the Trinity and the exploration of the meaning of Jesus the Christ – are not found explicitly in the Bible, but reflect the church's exploration of the Christian faith. Article VIII connects the tradition as expressed in the historic creeds with the authority of Scripture.

> *The Three Creeds, Nicene Creed, Athanasius's Creed, and that which is commonly called the Apostles' Creed, ought thoroughly to be received and believed: for they may be proved by most certain warrants of Holy Scripture. (BCP,* p. 701)

The Creed of St. Athanasius in the BCP (p. 695) is a long exposition of the meaning of the Incarnation and the Trinity but is seldom used in worship. For Anglicans, tradition is always developing as faith is defined for a particular age. Contemporary credal statements help us to explore who God is in language understandable today.

Reason

Reason is more than simply an intellectual activity. It is a kind of commonsense approach to the faith, which allows us to ask, "Does this make sense?" We believe that God has given us the gifts of reason and balanced judgment and that we are expected to use these gifts to understand and act upon God's call.

Anglicans generally take a non-literalistic approach to the Bible, using current scholarship and research to come to a deeper understanding. By using a lectionary, we commit ourselves to read the entire Bible, not just our favourite passages or those which avoid controversy. We explore Christian doctrine as we try to decide how the Christian faith is expressed in our own time and culture. We recognize that Christian doctrine is dynamic, open to interpretation, to be explored in the light of Scripture and tradition under the guidance of reason.

We use our reason to test our beliefs against our own experience and that of others. We believe that God is revealed in every age and culture. So the Anglican Church adapts itself to the language and culture and customs of the country where it is found. Churches use local music and instruments, vestments are made of local fabrics, and theology is written in terms understood by the particular culture.

Experience

Some Anglicans would add a fourth standard, that of human experience. Others would argue that reflection on experience is found in the interplay of reason and tradition, or reflection on past events.

Methodists describe these four standards of Scripture, tradition, reason, and experience as the "Wesley Quadrilateral." John Wesley, the founder of Methodism, lived and died as an Anglican priest and was influenced by the Anglican approach to theology, although his own conversion led him to emphasize in his preaching the importance of personal religious experience in Christian life.

Balancing the factors

How do we achieve a balance between all these factors? Anglicanism uses all of them to assess and evaluate our exploration of the faith.

Certainly we appeal to Scripture, tradition, and reason as we decide what is authoritative. We also look to the whole church community to help in making these decisions. We reflect on Scripture and tradition in the light of reason. It is the community that agrees on statements; it is the community's decisions which have official weight.

Ambiguity, variety, and flexibility

In the words of retired South African Archbishop Desmond Tutu, Anglicanism is a rather untidy system, but very, very lovable. It is not always easy to determine the Church's position on a particular matter or to define a single theological position or emphasis. The ambiguity of Anglican theology is its attempt to take into account the whole of our experience. A classic Anglican form of expression would be to say, "On the one hand... but on the other hand..." This is our strength and sometimes our weakness. Anglicanism is a way of thinking rather than a set of carefully defined conclusions.

Anglicans see doctrine as something that is not static, but is always changing and developing in new times and places. Richard Hooker, in the

The Laws of Ecclesiastical Polity, Book V. Ch. viii. 3, wrote, "The Church hath authority to establish that for an order at one time, which at another time it may abolish, and in both do well."

The liturgical texts of the Anglican Church accommodate divergent views. So Anglicans have developed an ability to live with diversity. Even within the Provinces of the Anglican Communion we have allowed that variety of views. Some Provinces of the Communion ordain women; some Provinces have decided against that ordination. Yet we have been able to exist within one family even though we cannot agree on all expressions of faith.

Common prayer

The community of the church meets regularly to worship together. When Anglicans come together to pray, their worship follows a particular pattern set out in our books of "common prayer." Language and customs may change from time to time and from place to place, but the basic pattern of the Eucharist and the Offices of Morning and Evening Prayer remain the same.

We agree to worship together according to a particular form, and priests at their ordination promise to conduct worship according to these authorized forms. We may add our individual prayers, silently or aloud, but we come together as a church to worship as a community. The forms of prayer are balanced, including penitence as well as praise. Within the unchanging prayers, there is room to express the particular concerns of this day or of this place.

These agreed-upon patterns of worship enable us to remain connected with other Anglicans even though we may have different theological views or may use different customs and gestures in worship. Evangelicals, Anglo-Catholics, charismatics – all worship according to the authorized texts. Our common worship roots and sustains us week by week.

The goodness of God's creation

Anglican prayers reflect our strong belief in the goodness of creation. Addressing God we pray, "You hate nothing that you have made." Nature is God's creation and is a source of God's revelation. Some people view the natural world as chaotic, or evil. But Anglicans believe that God has created us as part of that natural world and made us the stewards of creation. We have a responsibility then to look after the environment, the world God created as home.

Anglicans believe that the world, in the sense of society, is the proper sphere of action for Christians. We are not called out of the world but are called to take responsibility for the social order, to ensure that our society is a just and welcoming place for all people. Some people say that the church should not be involved in politics. The Anglican view has always been that Anglicans must take responsibility for the way society functions, and so it is right and proper for Anglicans to be involved at all levels of the political process. So Anglicans have made important contributions to Canada's political parties and to all levels of government. As a national church, we send briefs to governments and work with other denominations to see that Christian principles and concerns are clearly stated.

The Incarnation

In Jesus, God chose to become human and to share our life. As Stephen Sykes writes in *Incarnation and Myth*,

> *To be an Anglican means to belong to a church in which the story of the incarnation is repeatedly rehearsed and implied, in its liturgies, including its most recent revised service books... and in its Canon Law.* (p. 119)

The story of Jesus' life and death includes our own story. We are incorporated into the life and death of Jesus. We believe in the goodness of human life, created and redeemed by God. Some denominations are pessimistic about humanity, tending to believe that God is good but that human beings are sinful. Anglicanism holds an optimistic view of humanity. We believe that we are part of God's good creation. We are confident in God's grace, that God's plan is to bring us to our full potential as children of God. We have been redeemed and have received the gift of new life in our baptism.

Anglicans recognize the reality of sin and acknowledge that we need to repent and return to God's way. We rebel against God but we are not inherently evil. We affirm the reality of the atonement, that we are already redeemed by the death and resurrection of Jesus Christ. So our life is then a growing into the meaning of our baptism.

The trivial round

Anglicans believe that God is known to us in the daily routine of life. The Anglican hymn writer John Keble wrote, "The trivial round, the common task / Will furnish all we ought to ask" (*Common Praise*, #7). Daily routine is the road that takes us nearer to God. Anglicans favour pattern and order in worship, and enjoy framing their spirituality around the seasons of the Christian year – Advent and Lenten observances, saints days, festivals. We tend to place less emphasis on novelty and enthusiasm, and more on deepening established patterns of worship and observance.

The church

Some Anglican theologians have described the church as "the extension of the Incarnation." This description is another way of expressing the words of Jesus in John's gospel, "As the Father has sent me, so I am sending you." Anglicans believe that God calls the Church into being in order to do God's work. The Church is called to transform culture, to make the world a place where God may be known, and God's purpose fulfilled.

The sacramental principle

The goodness of God is expressed to humankind through physical creation. This is the same principle that leads us to see the goodness of the natural world, and to take seriously the life of the visible church. The principle is supremely illustrated in the Incarnation when God took our human (physical) nature. And it is this principle that Jesus hallowed in appointing bread and wine as the means for recalling his presence with us. God acts through the stuff of everyday life to communicate to us grace and power.

The Anglican way

So, yes, I believe that there is a distinctly Anglican way of doing theology, and I believe that it is based in large measure on our emphasis on the doctrines of Creation and Incarnation. We affirm that God created the world and humans as good, and we believe that God chose to come among us, to live and die as one of us, so that we might have new life in Christ. We affirm the importance of story and symbol and sacrament to remind us of God's presence. We believe that we are called into the community of the church, and into relationship with others as well as into relationship with God. Through the church, we learn the story of God's dealing with the community of faith, we join with other Christians to worship God, and we are strengthened to take the good news of the gospel to those outside the church.

Within the Anglican church, we have a wide tolerance for diversity. But we also affirm the standards of Scripture, tradition, and reason by which we test our beliefs. We have liturgical texts as articulations of belief. And we have a commitment to seek the common mind of the church through our systems of government in the life of the church.

8

How do Anglicans
make ethical decisions?

Anglicans apply the same three principles to their decision-making that they apply to theological exploration.

We appeal first to **Scripture**. Does the Bible have anything to say on this issue? How do we interpret what the Bible says, and what authority does it have for us? What biblical principles might assist us in making a decision? Anglicans do not hold a fundamentalist view of Scripture but examine it, contradictions and all, to arrive at a deeper understanding.

We appeal to the **tradition** of the Church. What have other Christians thought about the issues? How does Christian doctrine (creation, incarnation, redemption) illuminate the question for us? How is the issue affected by what we understand to be the nature of God and God's plan for the world? What official statements have been made by our church and others?

And we appeal to **reason**. Anglicans believe that God has given us our minds and expects us to use them to make decisions. Ethical decisions are seldom clear-cut. We must weigh the various alternatives and use reason to help us evaluate the evidence of Scripture, tradition, and our own experience.

We explore issues as part of a church community. So study groups and discussion can help us frame opinions on issues that confront us in our everyday life and work.

Over the years the Anglican Church has made a number of statements on particular ethical issues. These are not the opinions of individuals but are the considered judgment of a group – General Synod or its committees, or the House of Bishops. Thus they represent the common mind of the group at that particular time.

Birth control

The Lambeth Conference of 1920 warned "against the use of any unnatural means by which conception is frustrated."

By 1930, the bishops had come to a different point of view. While still stressing the importance of family life and parenthood as "the foremost duty" for married people, their report stated, "We cannot condemn the use of scientific methods to prevent conception, which are thoughtfully and conscientiously adopted." Birth control was not to be seen as a solution to unjust social and economic conditions. These social reforms should be tackled directly by the church.

In its report, Lambeth 1958 spent some time describing the purposes of marriage. In some Christian traditions, the primary purpose of marriage is the procreation of children. But the report said that the relationship of husband and wife and the place of stable family life in the nurture and care for all its members are equally as important. The words of the *BCP* marriage service (p. 564) remind us:

Marriage was ordained for the hallowing of the union betwixt man and woman; for the procreation of children to be brought up in the fear and nurture of the Lord; and for the mutual society, help, and comfort, that the one ought to have of the other, in both prosperity and adversity.

The Lambeth Conference in 1958 affirmed that family planning ought to be "the result of thoughtful and prayerful Christian decision." As a result, General Synod in 1967 urged the Government of Canada to make legal the dispensing of birth control information and means.

This is a good example of the way Anglican ethical decision-making takes place – over a long period of study and discussion, taking into account Scripture, tradition, current experience, and scientific knowledge.

Abortion

In 1967, the Anglican Church of Canada presented a brief to the Federal Standing Committee on Health and Welfare. It said,

> *We assert the general inviolability of the fetus and defend, as first principle, its right to live and develop. We lay the burden of proof to the contrary on those who, in particular cases, wish to extinguish that right on the ground that it is in conflict with another right having a greater claim to recognition. We recommend that the only grounds justifying abortion to which the criminal code should refer should be serious threat to the life or health of the expectant mother.*

In 1973, General Synod reaffirmed this position. While admitting the necessity of therapeutic abortion in special circumstances, the Synod rejected the principle of "abortion on demand." The 1980 General Synod again rejected the principle of "abortion on demand" or "for reasons of convenience or economic or social hardship," and committed itself to programs of education, counselling, and support for families.

In 1989, a news release affirmed the Anglican Church's position, that both the rights and needs of women and the rights and needs of the unborn require protection.

Abortion is a complex issue, not easily solved in absolute statements of right and wrong. As I understand it, the Anglican Church is saying that abortion is wrong. But sometimes the circumstances surrounding the pregnancy are also wrong, and we are called upon to make the best decision we can between two wrongs. As a church, we have a responsibility to help people make the best decision they can, and to provide education, counselling, and support.

Abortion must be seen as a community issue. We need to work to make our society a welcoming place for all children, and to work to correct economic and social injustices where they occur.

Capital punishment

Following a period of discussion by the House of Bishops and others, the General Synod of 1986 passed a resolution to inform the Prime Minister of Canada and the Minister of Justice "that it is opposed to the return of the death penalty." A pastoral letter from the House of Bishops set out the rationale for this decision, based on a belief in the sanctity of human life, on the inappropriateness of responding to violence with more violence, and on the need for Canadians to work for reform of the corrections system, to support both those who work within the justice system (police, prison guards, chaplains) and the victims of violence.

Early in the parliamentary debate on capital punishment, there appeared to be strong support for its return. I believe the representations that Canadian churches made to the Government of Canada influenced the decision not to reintroduce capital punishment.

Gambling

Gambling in various forms has increased in Canadian society to almost epidemic proportions. The lineups to purchase lottery tickets and the proliferation of casinos and bingo halls are all evidence of the spread of gambling in Canada.

As early as 1897, General Synod passed a resolution that it "deeply deplores the increasing evils of gambling and betting and would encourage the members of the Church... in every way to discountenance this practice."

The General Synods of 1946 and 1949 passed resolutions against gambling and the use of gambling to raise money for church purposes. The Synod of 1955 expressed its opposition to public lotteries and to the extension of gambling privileges. The national church newspaper adopted in 1983 a policy that rejected advertising from lotteries.

Since 1983 there has been no action or study at the national level, though some diocesan synods have had discussion on the subject and passed resolutions.

It seems to me that the general tenor of the debate in our church is against gambling as a means of fundraising for social and charitable purposes. There is no doubt, however, that some Anglicans do buy lottery tickets, go to casinos, and sell raffle tickets. Other Anglicans believe that it is wrong to depend for financial support on a system that often takes money from those who can least afford it. We need to share the responsibility for building a just society, rather than creating false hopes in people.

Drinking and dancing

While Anglicans deplore the abuse of alcohol, we have tended as a church to be more liberal in our attitude to social drinking. So you may find Anglican congregations hosting wine and cheese parties or permitting alcoholic beverages at parish gatherings.

This occasionally leads to interesting anomalies. For years, the Canadian Church Press, an organization of Canada's religious periodicals, refused to have a bar at its annual meetings. They had no objection, however, if the *Canadian Churchman* or the *Anglican Journal* had an open house that included a bar. And almost everyone attended!

Medical ethics

Many new medical techniques raise ethical questions: Should patients who are terminally ill have the right to choose the time and place of their own death? How long should life be prolonged? What are the implications of new discoveries in biotechnology? Should human embryos be frozen and the fetal tissue used to combat disease? What are the issues around surrogate parenthood or human cloning? The Human Life Task Force, established by General Synod in 2001, reflects theologically on the ethical issues involved and monitors ongoing developments in these areas.

Anglicans continue to study and reflect on these and other issues, using Scripture, tradition, and reason as guidelines for ethical decision-making. The Anglican Church of Canada has developed a code of ethics for those authorized to practice ministry in the church, and encourages dioceses to do the same. These and other documents may be found on the church's website.

Homosexuality

Along with many other denominations, the Anglican Church struggles with issues dealing with sexuality in general, and with homosexuality in particular. The Anglican Church includes many gay and lesbian clergy and lay people. In 1976, the House of Bishops set up a task force to advise them on matters related to homosexuality. In 1979, the bishops issued a statement "upholding the principle that Holy Matrimony is valid only between a man and a woman. Persons of homosexual orientation could be ordained but must commit themselves to a celibate lifestyle." (*Hearing Diverse Voices, Seeking Common Ground*, p. 4)

The bishops and others in the church continued to study the issue. In 1992, General Synod called upon the whole church to study homosexuality and homosexual relationships. A task force produced a study kit, *Hearing Diverse Voices, Seeking Common Ground,* that included material on the church's interpretation of Scripture, insights from modern scientific knowledge, and the experience of gay and lesbian people in our church. The Primate at the time, Archbishop Michael Peers, wrote in the preface to the study kit,

> *For many people in the church, as well as for many outside the church, this subject is new and somewhat frightening. But the Church has in scripture and tradition much to say about the issues involved – sexuality, inclusiveness, justice. The research of recent years is also valuable.*
>
> *But above all, at the heart of this discussion, there are persons created in the image of God and redeemed by our Savior's love, persons who are (sometimes unbeknownst to us) members of our own families and congregations.* (p. 3)

Many parishes across the country studied and reflected on the material. It was an opportunity for Anglicans to express their views and concerns. Anglican views on homosexuality and homosexual relationships probably reflect the whole gamut of opinion on this controversial topic. Whatever decisions we make as a church will cause pain and struggle for some. We wrestle with the issues and pray for God's guidance. We have been urged by the General Synod and by the Lambeth Conference to engage in study and dialogue, listening to the different voices of our fellow church members so that all points of view can be heard. I think that it is typical of our style of decision-making that we have spent a good deal of time studying this issue and have not rushed into a decision before Anglicans have had ample time to discuss it and reflect upon it. This has at times felt awkward; but because we are a church in which authority is widely dispersed, we need to involve many people at all levels in the church when making major decisions.

Decisions in the church have focused on the blessing of same-sex unions of persons civilly married. The General Synod of 2004 affirmed the value of respectful dialogue and the place of all baptized persons as members of the Anglican Church. It also affirmed "the integrity and sanctity of committed adult same-sex relationships."

The Primate's Theological Commission was asked to determine whether the blessing of same-sex unions was a doctrinal matter. This would determine the way in which a resolution allowing such blessings would be voted on by General Synod. (A doctrinal matter requires voting at two successive synods, while a non-doctrinal matter could be determined at one synod.) In 2007, following the St. Michael Report by this commission, General Synod resolved that "the blessing of same-sex unions is not in conflict with the core doctrine (in the sense of being credal) of the Anglican Church of Canada." (This was an important distinction as it opened the way for further discussion in 2010.) However, a resolution asking that any diocesan synod, with the concurrence of their bishop, be able to authorize the blessing of committed same-sex unions within that diocese was defeated by a narrow margin.

The General Synod of 2010 prepared a statement of its discussions on human sexuality. The statement affirmed the full inclusion of gay and lesbian members in the church, while acknowledging the variety of opinions held by faithful Anglicans. It acknowledged diverse pastoral practices in the dioceses and accepted a commitment to develop "generous pastoral responses" while declining to make a legislative decision. It urged continuing dialogue and study. Since that time, eight dioceses in Canada have passed motions permitting the blessing of same-sex unions as part of that pastoral response.

I have outlined in some detail the acts of General Synod to illustrate the way in which the Anglican Church of Canada makes decisions. As a church we continue to wrestle with this question. There are three factors to which we need to pay attention. There are issues of justice and inclusivity in our response to gay and lesbian members of our community. There is the decision of the federal and provincial governments to make legal the marriage of same-sex couples throughout Canada. We need to be responsive to the situation in our own country. And there is our commitment to walk together with other Anglican Provinces around the world. In Chapter 20, we explore some of the difficulties of being part of a family of churches where there is great diversity of understanding and practice, particularly regarding issues related to human sexuality.

Inclusivity

As a church, we need to be a welcoming community. So as Anglicans we are working to combat many of the "isms" of our culture – racism, sexism, ageism.

For many years, the Anglican Church of Canada has issued statements condemning **racism** and the victimization of visible minorities. The theme of the 1992 General Synod was multiculturalism and we celebrated the great variety of races and cultures that make up the Anglican Church of Canada. The staff and committees of General Synod regularly participate in anti-racism awareness training. Those concerned with worship look at ways in which the liturgy is enculturated, and use music, symbols, and prayers appropriate to each local culture. Individual parishes have sponsored refugees and helped them to become part of Canadian society. On the national level, the church works with governments and international agencies to bring justice to refugees.

The Anglican Church has among its members many First Nations and Inuit peoples. As a church, we have worked with them supporting land claims negotiations, and developing resources for ministry, listening to their wish to celebrate their identity within the community of the Anglican Church. As non-aboriginal peoples, we need to listen to and allow ourselves to be enriched by the gifts of aboriginal spirituality and tradition.

We need to oppose **sexism** and welcome both men and women into our churches at all levels. The ordained ministry of our church has been open to both men and women for 35 years, and we need to celebrate the gifts that ordained women have brought to the church. We need to ensure that women are well represented in the decision-making structures of the church.

In our new liturgies and hymns, we have tried to make our worship inclusive of men and women. So the masculine language of *The Book of Common Prayer* which refers to "all men" has been changed to more inclusive words such as "persons" or "people." We are also studying ways to use many of the feminine images found in the Bible when addressing God in prayers and hymns. We want to make our churches welcoming to people of all **ages**: children, teenagers, adults, the elderly. We need to be sensitive to each age group as we renovate our buildings, plan for worship, or provide programs for the parish. In recent years, we have seen two groups in particular being included more in worship – children and persons with physical disabilities. More and more of our churches have wheelchair access, for example. Similarly, children now play a greater role in worship.

Ecology

As Anglicans, we believe in the goodness of creation and in God's involvement in the stuff of everyday life. We believe that we are the stewards of creation, with a responsibility to care for this planet and for the creatures living within its natural systems. So we work for the care of our environment and for justice in social and economic issues. You can learn more about stewardship of our environment at the end of Chapter 6.

9

How do we relate to other churches?

On a Sunday night in January you will find Anglicans in churches big and small praying with other Christians during the Week of Prayer for Christian Unity. This celebration draws us to worship in one another's church buildings, to reflect on the call to unity, and to pray for the reconciliation of all Christians.

The Anglican Church is deeply committed to ecumenism, that movement within all the churches that fosters dialogue and cooperation. The word "ecumenism" comes from a Greek word meaning "the inhabited earth, the whole world." God created the world and is concerned for all creation. We are called by God to work for the unity, redemption, and reconciliation of the whole human race, because all people are created and loved by God. We live in a divided and suffering world and are called to bring healing and wholeness to all people.

With such convictions, the Christian church should be a sign of unity and hope to the world. But from the earliest centuries, the church has been divided by differences of belief and practice. This division weakens our witness to the world. Non-believers wonder how we can preach "One Lord, One Faith, One Baptism" and yet be divided, even hostile, towards each other.

Christian denominations do represent different lenses through which the faith is viewed. Sometimes denominations reflect the way that Christian belief has been expressed in particular cultural settings. The 20th century saw, however, a remarkable movement to draw together the churches in greater understanding and agreement, and that work continues.

Worldwide ecumenism

The modern ecumenical movement is usually dated from the Edinburgh Missionary Conference in 1910, though the earlier missionary movement of the nineteenth century and groups such as Bible Societies and the Student Christian Movement already emphasized interdenominational cooperation.

In 1927, the first World Conference on Faith and Order at Lausanne brought together Christians of many denominations to look at the doctrinal basis for the unity of the Church. Other meetings were held, leading eventually to the formation of the **World Council of Churches** in 1948.

The Anglican Church of Canada is one of 349 member churches, denominations and church fellowships, from more than 110 countries and territories. Canadian Anglicans have served as executive and staff and have played an important part in the life of the Assembly.

The World Council meets in full assembly every seven years. In 1983 the Assembly was held in Vancouver. The 9th Assembly was held in Porto Alegre, Brazil, in 2006. The 2013 Assembly will be held in Busan, South Korea. Some of the money from parish offerings supports the work of the WCC. The Council has no authority over its member churches but provides a forum for very diverse groups to meet and discuss the mission of the church. Member churches range from the Quakers with their silence in worship to the Orthodox churches with their elaborate liturgy; from sacramental churches, such as Anglicans, to the Salvation Army and the Church of Jesus Christ on Earth through the Prophet Simon Kimbangu (Zaire), which do not celebrate the sacraments at all. Work is carried on through three sections: Faith and Witness, Education and Renewal, and Justice and Service.

The Faith and Order Commission of the WCC provides theological support for the dialogue between churches. It includes Roman Catholics, although that church is not a full member of the Council. An important piece of the commission's work was the report *Baptism, Eucharist and Ministry* in 1982. The report was circulated to all churches and sets out a significant agreement between churches in these three areas. Despite differences in practice and emphasis, churches felt able to express some common understandings.

Canadian expressions

In Canada, Anglicans participate with many other denominations in the **Canadian Council of Churches**. Founded in 1944, the Council's 23 member churches represent 85% of Christians in Canada. Like the WCC, the Canadian Council provides a forum for dialogue and education, and a way for the churches to speak with one voice in Canadian society.

Canadian Christians do much of their work of social justice through coalitions whose membership represents many Christian denominations. This is an approach to social action which, I understand, is uniquely Canadian and one which the rest of the world has looked at with interest. KAIROS is one example of such a coalition. It unites 11 churches and religious organizations in action for human rights and justice, particularly ecological justice. Their work includes research, education, partnership and advocacy. Project Ploughshares is a coalition that focuses on peacemaking. Ecumenical organizations allow the participating churches to share ideas and resources and to present a united approach in advocacy to government and other groups.

Church to church

Anglicans also participate in bilateral discussions, or conversations with one other partner. These conversations take place internationally, funded by the Anglican Consultative Council; local conversations are funded through our contributions to the national church.

Relations between Anglicans and **Lutherans** have developed dramatically in recent years. In Canada, Anglicans and Lutherans have lived side by side for a century but have not always known each other well, as each church in the early days represented a particular ethnic heritage. Anglican-Lutheran dialogues at national and international levels came to a series of agreements which resulted in 2001 in a declaration of Full Communion between the Anglican Church of Canada and the Evangelical Lutheran Church in Canada (the Waterloo Declaration). This has allowed Canadian Anglicans and Lutherans to move towards greater recognition of members and ministry, Eucharistic sharing, and greater cooperation. Anglican priests can now serve as incumbents of Lutheran congregations and vice versa. The Anglican Church's website contains the guidelines for clergy serving in each other's churches.

The Anglican Church has ongoing discussions with the **Roman Catholic Church**, both locally and internationally. In 1981, the Anglican-Roman Catholic International Commission (ARCIC) submitted its final report, detailing discussions and areas of agreement on the Eucharist, ministry, and authority. In 1987, ARCIC II published a report on *Salvation and the Church*. Work continues on areas of mutual concern, in spite of some difficulties for Roman Catholics over the ordination of women to the priesthood and episcopate. The Canadian Anglican-Roman Catholic dialogue (ARC) celebrated its 40th anniversary in 2011.

On the international level we are in conversation with the **Orthodox** Churches, the **Oriental Orthodox** (Armenian, Syrian, Coptic, and Ethiopian Orthodox Churches) and the **Reformed** Churches (churches deriving from the Calvinist reforms of the sixteenth century).

In Canada we had a long period of dialogue with the **United Church of Canada**, beginning in 1943 and culminating in the preparation of a Plan of Union. More than 200 clergy and laity were involved in the various committees. In 1969 the Christian Church (Disciples of Christ) became participants in the discussion. In 1975 the plan was turned down by the Anglican Church. This was a sorrow and disappointment to many Anglicans. I had been a member since 1967 of the Doctrinal Commission, working on the theological basis for the union, and I felt sorry that those years of work had come to nothing.

But in retrospect I think that the church's decision was the right one. There was a time when merging several denominations into one large united church was the right approach. The United Church of Canada was formed by such a merger in 1925. On the Indian sub-continent, four united churches were formed in which Anglicans played a major role: the Churches of South India, North India, Pakistan, and Bangladesh. But, as time went on, union schemes foundered, frequently (it must be said) because Anglicans felt that they could not agree to the final arrangements.

I think that trends in ecumenism have moved away from organizational unions that result in large churches made up of several denominations. We now concentrate on cooperation and dialogue, and on common social action and sharing of resources, while respecting individual differences of belief and practice. We still need to work at getting to know each other, at working together whenever possible, at praying together. The Lund Principle, articulated at a WCC Faith and Order Commission meeting in Sweden in 1952, states that churches should do as much together as possible except where conscience prohibits such joint action.

Local ecumenism

Today Anglican parishes work together with neighbouring congregations in a variety of ways. Two inner city parishes, say Anglican and United, may work together to minister to low-income families and individuals who live in the community. Congregations invite others to attend worship services and education programs. Sharing summer services is popular. Sharing Sunday schools makes it possible to have larger classes and more teachers. In one town, the primary Sunday school class is taught in the Lutheran church and the junior class in the Anglican church.

Some Anglican parishes share a church building with a congregation of another denomination. They may worship separately but share office facilities and building expenses. In some places, there are shared ministries – congregations of more than one denomination who worship together and are served by a minister of one of the traditions. These arrangements are authorized by both denominations and the minister is responsible to both denominations for pastoral oversight. A shared ministries task group has representatives from Anglican, Lutheran, Presbyterian, and United Churches.

It is important for us to get to know our neighbours. Ecumenism involves listening to their stories and learning from them what God means in their lives. Ecumenism begins at the local level.

Years ago, when people spoke of "interfaith marriages," they meant that an Anglican had married a Roman Catholic or a Presbyterian. Other denominations were unknown quantities. There was even some doubt whether they were really Christian. Today, I am glad to be able to say, we have come a long way from that narrow parochialism.

We have had to. Rural depopulation means that many small churches can no longer afford to pay for seminary-trained stipendiary clergy of their own denomination. In the search to find alternative forms of ministry, working together with other churches in town is one option. People work together on community projects, curl or play hockey together, visit in each other's homes, very often are related. Coming together for worship may be a natural and right way to preserve the ministry and witness of the church in the local community.

In recent years we have expanded the idea of dialogue to include not simply other Christian denominations but also **other faith groups**. Canada's population has become much more diverse. The United Nations lists Toronto as the most multicultural city in the world and small towns are likely to have other world religions or faith groups represented. So all Christians are learning more about the customs and beliefs of our Jewish, Hindu, Muslim, and Buddhist neighbours. At the national level the Anglican Church is in conversation with other faith groups and is exploring ways in which we may come to understand each other better. *Occasional Celebrations*, a collection of special services, contains a rite for "the Celebration and Blessing of a Marriage between a Christian and a Person of Another Faith Tradition." Interfaith dialogue is a new area for many of us but, in our changing country, it is an important exploration.

The Anglican Church of Canada includes many **indigenous people**. Most of Canada's Inuit and many Indian people are Anglicans. Some worship in English; some have had the liturgy in their own language for a century or more. In the early days, the missionaries discouraged the use of Native language and customs in worship. Today Native and non-Native people are discovering the riches of aboriginal spirituality. The sense of the presence of God in the created world, the need for reverence for all God's creatures, and the importance of symbol and dance are some of the many gifts that First Nations people have to share with us.

10

How do we share the good news with others?

In 1988, the Lambeth Conference called upon the churches of the Anglican Communion to make the 1990s a Decade of Evangelism "with a renewed and united emphasis on making Christ known to the people of his world." (Lambeth resolution 43) The themes for the decade were to

proclaim the good news of the Kingdom;

teach, baptize, and nurture new believers;

respond to human need by loving service;

seek to transform the unjust structures of society;

care for the environment.

These have become known as the "marks of mission" and have been adopted throughout the Anglican Communion as a guide to mission.

This emphasis on evangelism included affirming the role of the laity in proclamation and mission, and recognizing the importance of equipping lay people for this work through education and training. During this period, most Anglicans saw a good deal of printed material about evangelism in the forms of prayers, study guides, newsletters, and articles. There were Institutes for Evangelism, weekend workshops, and courses of study, all designed to find ways to witness to the power of Jesus Christ to transform individuals and society.

The world today

Our world is a world of paradox. Modern forms of communication bring people closer together but also separate us. They make us aware almost instantly of conflict, hunger, and oppression, but we feel powerless to do anything. Technology simplifies much of our life but at the same time overloads us with information and tasks. Computers let us reach out to people around the world instantly, but keep us solitary in our offices. Families may enjoy a comfortable life style but pressures of work and other activities allow less time for relaxation and to be together. At one time in Canada, most people attended worship regularly. Religious organizations played an important role in people's lives. In the postwar years, churches were booming. Since then, church attendance has declined. Many people still list a church affiliation on the census form, but an increasing number feel comfortable listing "no religion." There are fewer people in church on Sundays or involved in church organizations and activities.

Yet there is in Canada today a great interest in matters of the spirit, and great hunger for spiritual understanding. Bookstores are full of volumes on psychology, understanding personality, discovering meaning, or combatting stress. All of these, though addressed in a secular way, reflect our deep desire to come to understand who we are, what life is all about, where peace and joy and meaning can be found. Formal church membership may be down, but the needs and hopes of human beings are as real and as urgent as ever.

What is evangelism?

The word "evangelism" comes from the Greek "good news." It is the same word as the Anglo-Saxon *god spel* or gospel.

Evangelism is proclaiming by word and action the good news of God in Jesus Christ. We offer the world a message of hope. That is, we believe that God created the world and sustains it and us. God sent Jesus to be born into our world and to take on the sufferings of the world, triumphing over evil by his death and resurrection. God is present and active in our world, through the power of God's Holy Spirit. God calls us to work for justice and peace for all, to help others to become the people God created them to be.

Anglicans tend to be a bit reticent about sharing their faith with others. Not for us the buttonholing of strangers and asking the dreaded question, "Are you saved?" Part of our awkwardness may be our shyness or embarrassment about asking and responding to such a personal question. Part of it is a good-mannered wish not to intrude into the privacy of others. But part of it, I am sure, is that for many people, it is the wrong question.

We recognize that there are many different kinds of religious experience. Some people may come to know Jesus through a dramatic conversion experience, so that they can pinpoint a particular time when their life changed. Others experience a gradual growing into the meaning of their baptism as they come to know more deeply who God is and what God's plan is for their life. So the confrontational language of a certain kind of evangelism may not be appropriate for either the speaker or the hearer.

My own experience is that I was always involved in the life of the church, sharing in its worship and community. Even as an adolescent, I remained connected and interested in the Christian faith. There have certainly been periods when my understanding has been challenged, when I have reassessed and deepened my faith. But the dramatic turnaround has not been part of my experience. Nor, I believe, should it be imposed as the only approach to evangelism. I think that there are as many ways to do evangelism as there are individuals.

Here are some of my beliefs about evangelism.

1. There is no one way to experience God in our lives, nor is there a single step-by-step plan that will enable every congregation to carry out an effective ministry of evangelism. We are all called to share the good news of who God is and how God is transforming the world. There are many different ways to do that sharing.

2. Evangelism is not about numbers. It is not a scheme to bring more people into the congregation. People may be drawn to our church life by the witness of Christian friends. But, if they are not, this is not in itself a sign that our evangelism has failed.

   Sometimes our witness to the gospel may even drive people away. When we denounce injustice and work for social change because we believe that the gospel requires this, some people may become angry and leave.

3. I find myself drawn to writings on evangelism that speak of it as a ministry of listening and hospitality. In this view, evangelism is not so much what you say to people, nor how you confront them with the claims of Jesus, but how you welcome them to the church, to your home, to your office. People are turned away from our churches by a frosty greeting, by unfamiliarity with the liturgy (all those books and papers that no one ever explains!), by the sense of an "inner ring" of members who don't seem interested in making room for newcomers. People are drawn to our churches by our hospitality, our genuine interest in them as persons, and the care with which we celebrate God's presence in our worship.

4. Evangelism is about telling our story and listening to the story of the other person. Howard Hanchey, an Episcopal (Anglican) priest and professor of Christian education, says in *Church Growth and the Power of Evangelism,*

    > *Many of us grew up with the notion that evangelism means telling our story, and getting others to believe what we believe...*
    > *Telling our story can be an important part of evangelism, but the ministry of introductions is better served by story-listening than by story-telling.* (p. 93)

    Listening allows us to affirm for others that they are important just as they are, that their lives have value, that their experiences have meaning. Everyone has a story to tell.

    Hanchey goes on to show us the next step. He suggests that, as listeners, we can gently help the storyteller to identify the turning points in their story, the places where God has been active in their lives. God does the work of conversion. Our job as evangelists is to celebrate and witness to God's presence in everyday life.

5. To be effective, evangelism needs to be rooted in the local setting, so much of the ministry to the world is done by lay members as they go about their daily work and recreation. The evangelistic work of the clergy is mainly done within the church building and among church members. Sometimes the role of clergy acts as a barrier to evangelism.

I know that strangers sometimes react differently when my husband is wearing his collar – more concerned about their language, more apologetic about their lapses, sometimes more argumentative.

Church should prepare lay people for their ministry of evangelism outside the church. Education in the faith, and training in the skills of listening and teaching are essential. The church needs to help lay people wrestle with what it means to be a Christian in particular job situations, in unemployment, at school, in illness or health, in affluence or poverty. God is transforming society, and calls us to share in that transformation. What do I need to learn in church in order to play my part in changing the world? As we are encouraged to reflect on the demands of the gospel in our own lives, then we are better equipped to help others explore these same issues.

6. Evangelism is action as well as words. We share in the work of evangelism when we give money to the Primate's World Relief and Development Fund, when we work for human rights/social justice with other Christians, when we serve meals at our community shelter, or contribute to the local food bank. The report of the Anglican Consultative Council in Wales 1990 *(Mission in a Broken World)* shares this story.

   *One Sunday in a village in Bangladesh a man went to church.
   He had never been before. Why did he go? He had attended
   the funeral of a member of the congregation and liked what
   he had heard said about the person. He knew he wanted to
   become that kind of a man and have similar things said about
   him when he died. This is the story of one man's journey into
   membership of his local church.* (p. 113)

People see our faith reflected in the way we behave. Our actions tell them what beliefs govern our lives. We do not know how we influence others; often a word or action that we barely remember turns out to have had a profound influence on someone else. A lifestyle based on the gospel is the best witness to the truth of the Christian faith.

11

What are the sacraments?

What is a sacrament?

The Catechism (*BCP*, p. 550) defines a sacrament as "an outward and visible sign of an inward and spiritual grace, given to us by Christ himself, as a means whereby we receive this grace, and a pledge to assure us thereof." In Baptism, by the outward and visible sign of water and the name of the Trinity, the inward and spiritual grace of cleansing and new birth are conveyed, and we are incorporated into the church, which St. Paul called "the Body of Christ."

The Latin word *sacramentum* meant oath, like a soldier's oath of allegiance. The word was used for the Greek *mysterion* ("mystery") in early Christian writings.

I referred to the "sacramental principle" at the end of Chapter 7. This is an important emphasis in Anglican theology and practice. We believe that God is revealed to us through the stuff of everyday life, through material things like bread and wine and water. So when we worship, we use our bodies; standing, sitting, and kneeling. We use our senses of touch and taste and smell. We believe that God's presence is made known to us in material ways.

Sacraments are an important part of Anglican spirituality. A sacrament operates on two levels, the seen and the unseen. God's gift of grace is expressed to us through material objects, transformed by God in order to strengthen us.

Sacraments are "effectual signs of grace" (*BCP*, p. 708). In the words of a popular catch phrase, they "effect what they signify." That is, they do not merely describe something but work to bring about what they describe. So

Baptism does not merely describe cleansing and new life, but actually brings about that new life in us as we receive the sacrament in faith. The Eucharist does not simply recount a past event (the death and resurrection of Jesus), but calls it into the present with all the force and power of the original event. The Eucharist actually brings about reconciliation and communion as well as describing it in words.

The Catechism speaks of two sacraments "ordained by Christ as necessary for salvation": Baptism and the Holy Communion. These are the two sacraments for which there is New Testament authority. When Jesus shares bread and wine with the disciples at the Last Supper, he says, "Do this in remembrance of me" (Luke 22:19). The last words of Matthew's Gospel command Jesus' followers, "Go therefore and make disciples of all nations, baptizing them in the name of the Father and of the Son and of the Holy Spirit" (Matthew 28:19).

The number of sacraments

The number of the sacraments was not defined until the Middle Ages. In early times, the Creeds and the Lord's Prayer were sometimes referred to as sacraments. By the 12th century, seven sacraments were listed: Baptism, Confirmation, the Eucharist, Confession, Unction (anointing of the dying), Orders (ordination), and Matrimony. Two of these – Baptism and the Eucharist – are almost universally accepted as sacraments. The Thirty-Nine Articles lists the other five as "commonly called Sacraments," allowed by the Scriptures but not having the same authority as the sacraments instituted by Jesus.

We Anglicans tend to define ourselves as distinct from either Roman Catholic or Protestant. We retain many elements of the Catholic tradition: the three-fold ordered ministry of bishops, priests, and deacons; the importance of the sacraments; the liturgical tradition of common prayer. We share with the Protestant churches a belief in the importance of Scripture and of the role of the laity in worship and government. But we did not come through the radical Protestant Reformation of the 16th century, and were only influenced in part by the Calvinist and Lutheran definitions of faith. As I have said earlier, we can find out better what Anglicans believe by looking at the words of our prayers rather than by examining a confessional statement or list of doctrines.

- In Confirmation we find the laying on of hands, along with prayer for the gift of an inward and spiritual grace.
- Ordination includes the laying on of hands with prayer for the gifts of the Spirit for particular ministries.
- The ministry to the sick and dying includes unction or anointing with oil blessed by the bishop, and may include the laying on of hands with prayer.
- Marriage includes the exchanging of vows and the giving of a ring to effect the union of the man and woman. The *BAS* speaks of their lives together as "a sacrament of [God's] love to this broken world" (p. 546).
- Reconciliation, or the private confessing of sin and the pronouncing of absolution by the priest, is not practiced a great deal in the Anglican Church, but is certainly available to all as a means of grace. The phrase used to describe this sacrament is "all may; none must; some should."

  Sacramental confession is a helpful spiritual practice for some and still has a place in our church. Some Anglican churches have a regular time for this sacrament, often on Saturday afternoon as a preparation for the Sunday Eucharist. The priest meets with penitents in the chapel or church.

In all of these services, we see that what is going on is something more than simply a collection of prayers. Some action takes place in each; some "outward and visible sign" is made by which "inward and spiritual" gifts are conveyed. We might contrast the seven rites with something like the funeral liturgy or Morning and Evening Prayer. Funerals and the Offices provide us with an ordered way to worship God, to bring comfort to others, to remember before God the needs of the church and the world. But these services do not use material objects and actions to bring about changes in us.

Whether we call all of them sacraments or not, the participants in the rites are changed in some way and God's gift of grace is given to them for specific purposes. As in many theological matters, Anglicans are careful not to define these things too closely!

12

What is the Eucharist?

There are differing opinions about the frequency of the Eucharist – oddly enough, both based upon a belief in the centrality of this service.

Because the Eucharist is so important, some Anglicans feel that it should only be celebrated infrequently and with a good deal of preparation. They might want to make their confession to a priest. They might want to prepare privately with an examination of conscience, prayers of confession, perhaps some reading that might help them to feel ready to take part in this sacrament. Some Anglicans like to come fasting to Communion, and so wait until there is an opportunity to participate in an early morning Eucharist.

Other Anglicans believe that, because the Eucharist is so important, it should be celebrated as often as possible, and some parishes have daily celebrations. During the 20th century, Anglicans gradually moved to more frequent celebrations of the Eucharist and it is now the central service on a Sunday in many parishes. This service has many names, each reflecting a particular emphasis and meaning.

- **Eucharist:** A Greek word meaning thanksgiving. We give thanks for God's gift of new life through the life, death, and resurrection of Jesus Christ.
- **Lord's Supper:** The Christian family meal, instituted by Jesus at the Last Supper which he shared with the disciples. We follow Jesus' command recorded in Luke 22:19, "Do this in remembrance of me..."
- **Holy Communion:** A solemn event, which brings us closer to God and to each other. It is a sacrament that we share with each other in community.

- **Mass:** From the final words of the traditional Latin text: *Ite, missa est* – "Go, you have been sent." Jesus sends us out into the world to carry the good news into our daily lives. The Eucharist is not just for our own comfort; it is meant to strengthen us for witness in the world. The word "Mass" is less common in Anglican circles, but we do retain its use in "Christmas" – the "Christ Mass," giving thanks that God took flesh and came to live among us.

As a sacrament of the church, the Eucharist allows God's grace to come to us through tangible and natural elements – bread, wine, water. So we present at the altar bread and wine, representing the fruits of our daily life and work. Sometimes the bread and wine are on a small table (the credence table) near the altar until the altar is prepared at the time of the Offertory. Sometimes the bread and wine are brought by members of the parish (children too!) to the altar at the offertory.

This action reminds us that we bring these gifts to represent the daily life and work of the entire congregation. A prayer used in England at the time bread and wine are offered says,

Blessed are You, Lord God, Creator of all things. Through Your goodness we have this bread to offer, which earth has given and human hands have made. It will become for us the Bread of Life.

Blessed are You, Lord God, Creator of all things. Through Your goodness we have this wine to offer, fruit of the vine and work of human hands. It will become our Spiritual Drink.

We receive back again the bread and wine, transformed by God's spirit into vehicles for sharing Christ's love with us.

God comes to us through the things of everyday life, like bread and wine. Anglican churches often use small wafers of unleavened bread – which taste something like rice paper but which make the administration of Communion to the people more convenient. But many churches prefer to use ordinary bread, usually in the form of a small bun or loaf. We use fermented wine, drunk from a common cup or chalice. The one loaf and the one cup are important symbols of our communion, our **one-ness** in the Body of Christ.

Anglicans deliberately have never defined too closely what happens to the bread and wine in the Eucharist, but there are two classic views of what happens at the prayer of consecration. One view is that the bread and wine are changed, to become in some way the body and blood of Christ. The other view is that the Eucharist is a recalling of the Last Supper and a remembrance of Jesus' death and resurrection. *The Book of Common Prayer* states both these views in the sentences used for administering the sacrament (page 84).

"The Body of our Lord Jesus Christ, which was given for thee, preserve thy body and soul unto everlasting life." This sentence represents the first view, that the bread and wine have somehow been changed into the body and blood of our Lord.

"Take and eat this in remembrance that Christ died for thee, and feed on him in thy heart by faith with thanksgiving." This sentence views the Eucharist as memorial, as recalling the final events of Jesus' earthly life. It recalls the past event in a way that brings the power and meaning of the event into our lives. We believe that Jesus' death and resurrection will inform our lives and preserve our bodies and souls "unto everlasting life."

I said earlier that we can tell what Anglicans believe by the way we worship. Our practice at Communion gives us an important clue about what we believe happens at the consecration of the bread and wine. Anglicans never take the consecrated bread and wine and simply return them to the cupboard. *The Book of Common Prayer* is very clear:

> If any of the consecrated Bread and Wine remain, the Priest and other Communicants shall reverently eat and drink the same. (p. 86)

The Book of Alternative Services says,

> Any remaining consecrated bread and wine (unless reserved for the communion of persons not present) is consumed at the end of the distribution or immediately after the service. (p. 184)

Unconsumed bread and wine may be set aside in a special place to be brought to the sick and shut-ins. Here our terminology is sometimes confusing. We call the whole celebration the "sacrament" of the Eucharist. But we also use the term "sacrament" to refer to the consecrated bread and wine. So we speak of taking the sacrament to shut-ins, and we talk about the "reserved sacrament," or the bread and wine set aside in a special place, usually a wall cupboard called an "aumbry," near the altar. This reverence for the elements of Communion shows that Anglicans believe that in some way the bread and wine, which have been presented at the offertory and have been broken and blessed at the prayer of Consecration, have been changed and become in some special way the sacramental presence of Christ. The elements cannot be treated casually.

When Queen Elizabeth I was asked her opinion of Christ's presence in the sacrament, she is said to have replied,

'Twas God the word that spake it,
He took the Bread and brake it;
And what the word did make it;
That I believe, and take it.

We do not define too closely what happens. But our practice indicates that we believe that, in the Eucharist, God is present to us. We believe also that we ourselves are changed and strengthened as we receive the Bread of Life.

The service

The Book of Alternative Services describes the Eucharist as follows. This pattern is now found in the Eucharistic rites of most Christian churches. *The Book of Common Prayer* Communion service includes the same elements, though arranged in a slightly different order.

The gathering of the community

We are called from our separate lives to join together as the Christian Community. It is the particular duty of those who are ordained priests to gather the Christian community, and to lead the people in worship. So the priest who is presiding at the Eucharist greets the community and helps us gather our thoughts and prayers in the opening Collect and in appropriate songs and canticles.

The hymn "Glory to God" is appropriate in the joyful seasons of the year, or another hymn of praise may be sung. The *Kyrie Eleison* ("Lord Have Mercy") and the *Trisagion* ("Holy God") are appropriate in the penitential seasons of Advent and Lent.

The proclamation of the Word

Readings are taken from the Old Testament (the Hebrew Scriptures)[1], the Psalms, the Epistles or other New Testament passages, and the Gospels. Every Sunday we hear a good deal of Scripture read. Sometimes we can hear the words of Scripture as if they are addressed directly to us. At other times, we hear an incident in the life of the Hebrew people or the early church and we realize that this is part of "our" story too.

It is important for us to know our story as people of God. The sermon gives the preacher an opportunity to reflect on the meaning of the words we have heard. It should be brief and should connect the readings to our life of faith today. We sum up our belief by reciting together the Creed, our statement of faith. Most often in the Eucharist we use the Nicene Creed, a statement of the Christian faith dating from the 4th and 5th centuries. It begins "**We** believe" because it was a statement prepared by a council of Christians. The Apostles' Creed is older. It is the baptismal creed of the early church, and dates from the 4th century. It begins "**I** believe" because it is affirmed by each baptismal candidate in making a declaration of faith before baptism.

---

1. Some Christians prefer to use the term Hebrew Scriptures to describe that historic section of the Bible. This is out of respect for the Jewish people, for whom the terms "Old" and "New" Testaments may imply a judgment on God's revelation. In this book, I use the terms "Old" and "New" Testaments as those are the terms which are used in Anglican liturgical books.

The prayers of the people

These prayers are usually led by a deacon or lay member of the community. Together we pray for the church, the world, ourselves, those in need, and those who have died. The prayers should reflect the needs and concerns of this particular community, but should also direct our attention outwards to God's world. The *BAS* contains many forms of intercession and thanksgiving, or the prayers may be drafted by the leader.

Confession and Absolution

If penitential prayers were not used at the beginning of the service or in the Prayers of the People, then a form is provided for the confession of sin and the pronouncing of the absolution by the priest.

The Peace

As we conclude this section of the Eucharist, the priest greets us with the phrase, "The peace of the Lord be always with you." We may be invited to turn and extend that greeting to our fellow worshippers. The greeting is an affirmation of our oneness in Christ and a sign that we have been reconciled to God and to one another.

The exchange of the Peace is a return to a custom of the early Church. Initially some Anglicans found this difficult. We had not been accustomed to shaking hands with our neighbours during the service, and some felt that this broke for them the solemnity of worship.

It is important to remember that the exchange of the Peace is a liturgical act. It is part of the worship service. So it is not a time for wild hugging (though there may be occasions where that is appropriate!) nor is it necessary to greet individually everyone in church (though in a small congregation, that may be quite appropriate). The passing of the peace is a ritual action indicating that the service of the Word has concluded, that we have heard and reflected on the Scriptures, prayed for ourselves and the world, and confessed our sins and received assurance of God's forgiveness. Now, forgiven by God and reconciled to one another, we prepare to begin the Great Thanksgiving.

I think it is important to treat others gently at this point in the service. Those who are passing the Peace need to be sensitive to the quiet reticence of some in the congregation. And those who prefer a less exuberant style of greeting ought not to snarl at their fellow worshippers!

The celebration of the Eucharist

Dom Gregory Dix, in his classic work *The Shape of the Liturgy,* describes the "four-action" shape of the Eucharist: Jesus **took** bread, **blessed** it, **broke** it, and **gave** it to the disciples. In the liturgy these actions can be seen in

1. **The Offertory.** Bread and wine are brought to the altar.
2. **The Prayer.** The people, through the words and actions of the presider, give thanks to God over the bread and wine.
3. **The Fraction** (which means "breaking"). The bread is broken.
4. **The Communion.** Bread and wine are distributed to the congregation. (pp. 48 ff)

The offertory

Members of the congregation bring gifts of bread and wine forward to the altar, along with our gifts of money. Sometimes the bread and wine are set on a small table or shelf (called the credence table) beside the altar, and are moved by the priest, deacon, or servers to the altar at the offertory. The Prayer over the Gifts changes each Sunday to reflect the theme of the day.

These gifts represent our daily life and work. God gives us many gifts. We return to God the offering of our whole lives. As the bread and wine are taken in order that they may become the sacramental presence of Christ for us, so God takes our lives in order that we may become expressions of the life of Christ in the world.

The Great Thanksgiving

The Eucharistic prayer is a prayer of thanksgiving for God's gifts to us in nature, in the history of God's people, and, above all in the coming of Christ to our world. Following ancient Hebrew custom, we bless the bread and wine by giving thanks over them.

The prayer begins with praise and thanks to God for the history of the people of God, for all those events when God's presence and care were made known to us. We rehearse the story of creation, of God's revelation to us in the lives of Abraham and Sarah, of Moses, of the prophets. We praise God by saying or singing the words of a beautiful and ancient hymn known as the *Sanctus* ("Holy, holy, holy Lord").

The prayer then goes on to tell the story of the life, death, and resurrection of Jesus, focusing particularly on the words that Jesus said over the bread and wine on the night he was betrayed. This is the core of the prayer, in which we remember Christ's action and join ourselves with it. This section of the Eucharistic prayer is usually followed by a paragraph known as the *anamnesis*, a Greek word which means literally "not forgetting." That is, we are careful not to forget Christ's suffering, death, resurrection, and ascension. And this is not simply the recalling to mind of an action long past, but it brings into the present that past act with all its power to change.

We ask God to send the Holy Spirit upon this offering of the Church. This is called the *epiclesis*, meaning "to call down upon." We ask God to strengthen us that we may become one body in Christ.

The congregation joins in the saying of the Lord's Prayer, as a summary and assent to all that has been said. A silence follows the Lord's Prayer as this brings us to the end of the Great Thanksgiving. It is a moment to be quiet in the knowledge of Christ's sacramental presence, and to prepare ourselves for receiving Holy Communion.

The breaking of the bread

This is the third action of the Eucharist. As the preacher earlier in the service took the written word of Scripture and broke it open for the nourishment of the people, so now the presider breaks the bread in order that it may feed all the communicants. We, though many, share in the one Bread which is Christ.

The Communion

We come to the altar to receive the sacramental gifts, now blessed by God to strengthen us and to nourish us with the life of Christ. We join with our fellow Christians and express our unity in Christ.

The usual Anglican custom is to receive the bread in our cupped hands and to bring the hands directly to the mouth. Our custom is to drink from a common chalice or cup as a sign that we are one body. Because of the number of serious epidemics of flu or respiratory viruses in recent years, many dioceses now forbid the practice of receiving Communion by "intinction" – that is, by dipping the wafer or piece of bread into the chalice. If you prefer not to drink from the common cup, receiving only the bread is sufficient.

People may receive Communion either kneeling or standing. Those who kneel do so with a sense of reverence for the solemn act in which they are sharing. Those who stand to receive do so from a sense of thanksgiving that God comes to us in the sacrament. This is a very ancient tradition. The Council of Nicaea in 325 AD said that Christians do not kneel on Sunday because it is the Lord's Day. On that day we can stand in God's presence as children and not slaves.

Either posture is appropriate. At one time, Anglicans knelt to pray and stood to sing. Today we stand much more frequently in worship as a sign of praise and thanksgiving. This change in posture reflects a recovery of the practice of the early centuries when Christians stood for much of the worship service.

Prayers after Communion and dismissal

The post-Communion prayer is specific to the Sunday and is found with the Collect and other prayers of the day. It may be concluded with the doxology or other prayers. The service concludes with the dismissal. This is a particular historical ministry of the deacon. The deacon's job is to connect the worship of the Church to our daily work in the world. Therefore the deacon, if there is one present, sends the people out to their daily ministries. A blessing may be said.

When the service ends, our Christian life, strengthened by the Eucharist, begins. We are sent out from our worship into the world to "love and serve the Lord" and to share the good news of Jesus Christ with others.

13

How do we become members of the Church?

Christian Initiation is the term we give to the process by which we become members of the Body of Christ, incorporated into the family of the Church. The rites by which we celebrate this are Baptism and Confirmation.

Baptism

The Anglican Church celebrates Baptism in many different ways. The traditional picture involves small babies in white christening gowns surrounded by parents and godparents. But increasingly, this picture is changing as adults, older children, and teens come forward as candidates for Baptism.

At one time in Canada, baptism was not a public sacrament. Baptisms took place on a Sunday afternoon with only the immediate family and godparents present. Sometimes the service seemed merely a prelude to a large tea party celebration.

In the last 30 years though, scholars have helped us come to a new understanding of the meaning of baptism and the important role it plays in the life of the whole congregation. We recognize now that baptism is not simply a personal rite for the cleansing of sin in the child. Nor is it some sort of superstitious protection against disease and death that has to be done before the infant is too old.

Rather, baptism is a corporate act, by which the individual becomes part of the Christian community and is given the gift of new life. So, if this is a community event, then it is important that baptism be celebrated with the community present to support and receive this new member.

Both the *BAS* and the *BCP* speak about the importance of Baptism taking place at a public service, and the *BCP* includes a form of reception in which the congregation welcomes publicly those who have been privately baptized (that is, those baptized in emergencies [p. 542]). The *BAS* suggests certain Sundays which are particularly appropriate for baptisms: Easter (especially at the Vigil, the evening before Easter Sunday), Pentecost, All Saints, the Baptism of the Lord, and any Sunday when the bishop is present.

In the early church, the bishop presided at all baptisms. As the church grew and it was no longer possible for the bishop to be present at every baptism, this responsibility was delegated to priests. But the presence of the bishop reminds us that our baptism makes us members not just of this congregation, nor of the Anglican Church, but of Christ's holy church (*BCP*, p. 523).

Baptisms normally take place in the church, though they may take place in a hospital in an emergency. A lay person may baptize in an emergency but, at a later time, the baptism must be registered in the parish church. If the baptized person recovers, then both the *BCP* and the *BAS* provide forms of service by which the baptized person is received into the life of the congregation.

Baptisms take place at the font, a large bowl into which water is placed. This may be a fixed piece of furniture, often located near the door of the church as a sign that it is by Baptism that we enter into membership in the church. Or it may be portable and placed at the front of the church for the service so that all present can witness the Baptism. Sometimes an infant may be totally immersed in the water. Most often, Baptism is done by pouring water three times over the forehead of the candidate.

The Baptism service

The service begins with prayers and the reading of Scripture. The candidates for Baptism are then presented. Infants and young children are presented by parents and sponsors (often called godparents) who make promises on behalf of the infant.

In the early church, Baptism was for adults, who were baptized at the Easter Vigil after a lengthy period of preparation that took months or even years. The children of Christian parents could also be baptized because of the faith and commitment of their parents. Later, as Christians became more numerous, the baptism of infants became the more popular custom.

Baptism is incorporation into the Christian family. So the Anglican Church, along with a number of other Christian denominations, baptizes infants and small children when other Christians are willing to make the baptismal promises on their behalf.

Older children, youth, and adults are presented by sponsors but make the promises for themselves. Though the wording of the questions is somewhat different in our two liturgical books, the candidates promise basically the same thing: to renounce evil, to turn to Jesus, and to obey Jesus as Lord. The congregation joins with the candidates in reciting the Apostles' Creed, the ancient baptismal creed of the early church. Thus we affirm together our common faith. *The Book of Alternative Services* is more explicit in seeing this as a reaffirmation of baptismal vows on the part of all present, because it goes on to ask the congregation to make a series of promises that draw out the implications of the baptismal covenant. We promise to continue in the apostles' teaching and fellowship, a promise to join our life with that of this worshipping community. We promise to resist evil, to proclaim by word and example the good news of God in Christ, to seek to serve Christ in all persons. And we promise to strive for justice and peace among all people.

By Baptism we are not called simply to a personal faith in Jesus or membership in the church, but also to a life of service to others, to evangelism, to action for justice and peace.

The Baptism itself

Water is an essential element in baptism. (In Anglican churches, the water is generally poured into the font so that the congregation can see and hear it.) The theme of water recurs in many places in Scripture, and the baptismal prayers refer to some of them:

- In Genesis, the Spirit broods over the waters of Creation;
- In the Exodus, the Hebrew people are led from bondage into freedom through the waters of the Red Sea;
- Jesus is baptized in the Jordan River.

Water is life-giving; it is essential for sustaining life. Without it, we die. We float in the water of the womb before we are born; in baptism, we are born to new life in Christ. Water symbolizes cleansing; in baptism we are cleansed and delivered from sin. We go down into the water to die with Christ; we are raised with Christ to new life.

In Baptism, we are given a name. Each candidate is presented by name and the name is repeated as part of the actual baptism. Names are important. They represent our uniqueness as individuals. They identify us and describe us to others. When our names are misused by others, we feel as though our whole person is threatened. In Baptism we are given a name that identifies us as an individual, a member of Christ, and a child of God.

Baptism is done in the name of God the Trinity. The baptismal formula says, "I baptize you in the name of the Father, and of the Son, and of the Holy Spirit." This formula is almost universally used by Christian denominations. Today some people are concerned about the use of exclusively masculine imagery for God. Talking about God as Father creates some difficulties for them. Sometimes people have very bad memories of their own fathers, and using "Father" as an image for God creates a barrier that they have to work to overcome. Sometimes people also wish to enrich our understanding of who God is by looking at some of the other images for God in Scripture: God as mother hen and mother eagle, as housewife looking for a lost coin, as mother, as Lady Wisdom. So there have been suggestions for new ways to name the persons of the Trinity: Creator, Redeemer, and Sanctifier; Source of all being, Eternal Word, and Holy Spirit. But often these other ways of naming God seem to be merely job descriptions of what God does. They lack a personal dimension. Although they expand our images for God, they do not always convey the sense of the Trinity as a relationship between persons. So Anglicans continue to affirm the use of the traditional Trinitarian formula as part of the requirement for Baptism, while at the same time expanding our images of God in other prayers.

In Baptism, the celebrant marks the sign of the cross on the forehead of each candidate. Oil blessed by the bishop may be used. The newly baptized may receive a candle, usually lit from the Paschal or Easter candle, as a sign that in Baptism they have passed from darkness to light. Prayer is made for the gift of the Holy Spirit.

The congregation welcomes the new baptized into "the household of God" and invites them to share in the life of the faith community and in the responsibilities of membership in Christ.

Confirmation and Holy Communion

In the early years of the church, when the bishop presided at all baptisms, the rite included both baptism and confirmation (the laying on of hands with prayer for the gift of the Holy Spirit). As numbers of Christians increased, and the bishop could no longer be present at all baptisms, the rite of baptism was given over to priests. The post-baptismal ceremony of laying on of hands and anointing was delayed until the candidates could come before the bishop.

In the Eastern churches, oil consecrated by the bishop was used by the priest to complete the rite of initiation. In Orthodox churches today, baptism, anointing, and first communion are part of a single rite for infants or adults. In the Western Church, baptism of infants came to be the norm and confirmation was delayed until a later age.

For hundreds of years, Christians continued to receive Communion before Confirmation. But gradually Christians received Communion less and less frequently and children no longer received the sacrament. It became the custom for children to undergo a period of preparation and instruction in the faith and to be confirmed before they could receive Communion. *The Book of Common Prayer* has a direction to that effect.

In recent years, the church as a whole has done a good deal of reflection about the meaning of Christian Initiation. This has led many denominations to change a number of practices. Specifically, the Anglican Church came to an understanding that Baptism conveys full membership in the church. This allows us to recognize baptized members of other denominations as full members of the one church of Jesus Christ. So we allow all who are baptized to receive Communion at Anglican services.

But this permission immediately created a problem within Anglican churches. If we could permit visiting Lutherans or United Church members to receive Holy Communion in our churches because we affirmed their baptism, how could we deny admission to Holy Communion to our own Anglican children, baptized into the church and regularly attending worship with us?

In 1968, the Lambeth Conference gave permission for baptized children to be admitted to Communion after a period of instruction suitable to their age. Meetings of the Anglican Consultative Council in 1984 and 1987 supported this practice. A number of Anglican Churches around the world, including the Anglican Church of Canada, have adopted the practice. In Canada, we have excellent resources for the preparation of children and parents for Communion, including *Life in the Eucharist*.

At first the custom of children receiving Communion seemed strange to many Anglicans. But I think what made many of us support this practice was the experience of the children themselves. Many children felt excluded when they came to the altar rail with their parents and received only a blessing. Many priests sorrowed over having to refuse the outstretched hands of children at the rail. Children are eager to share in the family meal, to join with the congregation in the fullness of our worship. Here are some comments from parents and children:

When children can share in the Eucharist, the family is complete in every way. (parent)

It's Jesus' body and blood. I feel good because I'm sharing some of Jesus. It makes me part of him. (age 8)

I feel happy. It means giving. (age 6)

Sometimes adults have felt that children need to **understand** what the Eucharist means in order to share in it. But how many adults understand or can express all that the Eucharist means? This sacrament is the family meal by which all the baptized are fed and strengthened for everyday life. Children are part of that family, and need to share with us in that meal.

Confirmation

What then is the place of Confirmation, now that it is no longer the rite that admits us to Holy Communion?

The nature of Confirmation and its relationship to Baptism has never been clearly defined in Anglican theology. Some Anglican theologians believe that the fullness of the Spirit is given in Baptism; no further rite is necessary. Others argue that Baptism is somehow incomplete without Confirmation, Some say that Baptism makes us full members of Christ but Confirmation gives us gifts of the Spirit to strengthen us for adult ministry and responsibility in the church.

In *The Book of Alternative Services*, there are three prayers for the solemn renewal of commitment to Christ, made in the presence of the bishop. One is for Confirmation, calling for the gift of the Holy Spirit to strengthen and empower. The second is for Reception, receiving into the fellowship of the Anglican Church a member of another denomination who has already been confirmed. The third prayer gives the opportunity for the formal Reaffirmation of Baptismal Vows before the bishop.

14

How do we celebrate our family life?

We are baptized and become part of the family of faith. But we are also part of a network of family relationships from our earliest childhood to our present life. The church has a number of rites to help us celebrate events and relationships in our family life.

Weddings

A wedding is a joyful occasion in the life of a family. If the bride and groom are members of the parish, the wedding becomes a celebration for the church family as well. Anglican weddings may be large elaborate services with many guests, lots of music, and the celebration of the Eucharist. Or they may be simpler.

Let's look at how we prepare for a wedding according to Anglican custom, and how we celebrate this happy occasion.

Before a wedding

First, the bride and groom contact the parish priest and establish a wedding date that is convenient for them, for the parish, and for the officiating minister. (Often, the date is determined primarily by the availability of the right hall for the reception following the wedding ceremony.) Some time must also be spent answering questions and filling out documents.

Before any wedding can take place, the church requires some specific preparation over a period of time. The Anglican Church normally requires at least 60 days' notice. Sometimes the priest sees the couple for several meetings. Sometimes other couples in the parish take responsibility for preparing those about to be married in the church. Sometimes the bride and groom join with other couples in the diocese for a marriage preparation course.

The purpose of this kind of preparation is to help the bride and groom understand each other better, and to begin discussion on some of those areas which often cause disagreement in families. The couple is encouraged to explore their family backgrounds and expectations. How will they celebrate holidays? What are their expectations about elderly relatives, and how will they share life with their extended families? How do they like to spend or save money? How will they spend their spare time? What life goals do they have? The aim of these questions is to open up areas for discussion and help get the new marriage off on a realistic footing. The groom may assume that when his parents are elderly, they will naturally come to live with or near his family. This possibility may never have crossed the bride's mind!

Because the church building is home to the parish family, there are a number of church regulations that apply when people come to get married. Canon XXI, "On Marriage in the Church," is a regulation of General Synod and so governs the practice of marriage in the Anglican Church of Canada. ("Canon" is one of those words with several meanings for Anglicans. Here it means a set of laws passed by General Synod that govern life in the Anglican Church of Canada.) There may also be diocesan canons and parish customs which determine what customs are permitted. And there are, of course, a number of civil regulations required by the province in which the wedding takes place.

Priests who officiate at weddings do so as official representatives of the Anglican Church of Canada and of their diocese. But they are also representatives of the civil authority of the province. Each priest must be registered with the appropriate government department and receives an identification number which appears on all the signed documents. These forms are returned to the government immediately following the wedding to register the marriage. Priests are obliged to meet all church and civil requirements.

As the couple will be exchanging vows in a Christian ceremony, they will also be encouraged to look at the Christian understanding of marriage and family life. A realistic acceptance of the complexities of married life plus the strength and support of active Christian faith will give the couple a good start in building a permanent, happy marriage. The seriousness with which the Church takes the marriage vow is evident in the words:

- forsaking all other, keep thee only unto her/him, so long as you both shall live. (*BCP*, p. 565)
- forsaking all others, to be faithful to her/him so long as you both shall live. (*BAS*, p. 543)

These are promises made before God and the community for a lifetime.

At one time, "banns" were called in church, asking the community to come forward if they knew of any impediment to the marriage. In less mobile societies, when most people lived in small communities, calling the banns in the parish church was considered a good way to prevent bigamy or other illegalities! Now civil law in many provinces requires the couple to obtain a marriage licence. But Anglican couples may still have the banns called in their parish church if they wish to follow that custom.

When marriages break down

The Church also recognizes that, even with the best hopes and intentions, marriages do break down for a variety of reasons. So the revision of the Marriage Canon in 1968 was designed to address that pastoral situation and to permit the remarriage of divorced persons in church. The church recognizes that couples come to a second marriage with serious intent and are looking to the church to bless the solemn vows which they are making. All couples must complete a program of preparation before marrying in the church. In the past, an application for permission to remarry had to be made by the priest on behalf of the couple to a Marriage Commission of the diocese or larger jurisdiction. The lawyers, clergy, and lay people on this Commission examined the application and the legal documents of the divorce(s), and then ruled on whether or not the marriage might take place in the church. The work of these Commissions has been done away with. A resolution of General Synod in 2004 states that the incumbent of a parish may grant permission to remarry if satisfied that the previous marriage has been legally dissolved, and that the couple understands the nature of Christian marriage and is prepared to enter into and sustain the new marriage. A bishop may appoint a Matrimonial Officer or other individual who may be consulted if there are questions. Each diocese has guidelines governing its marriage discipline.

Interdenominational and interfaith marriages

In the Anglican Church of Canada, a marriage cannot be celebrated between two persons who have not been baptized. If one person is baptized and the other is not, then the permission of the bishop must be sought before the wedding can take place in church.

Where the bride and groom come from different denominations, it is appropriate for the minister/priest of the other denomination to participate in the wedding service in some way. The priest who hears the vows is the one deemed to be the officiant at the wedding and responsible for the legal documents.

There is a set of guidelines governing the marriage between Anglican and Roman Catholic partners. You may obtain a copy of "Pastoral Guidelines for Interchurch Marriages Between Anglicans and Roman Catholics in Canada" (Publications Service CCCB, 1987) from the Anglican priest or the diocesan office. These guidelines were agreed upon by Anglican and Roman Catholic bishops in 1987.

Occasional Celebrations[1] contains a rite for the celebration of interfaith marriages (page C31); those between an Anglican and, for example, a Hindu, Buddhist, Jew, or Muslim. This is called "Marriage Between a Christian and a Person of Another Faith Tradition." Again, the priest needs to seek permission from the bishop for the marriage to take place in the church. The service needs to be sensitive to the faith and concerns of the non-Christian party, yet also needs to preserve the integrity of the Christian view of marriage in the Christian place of worship.

---

1. Texts from *Occasional Celebrations* are also available on the Anglican Church of Canada website www.anglican.ca.

The place of the wedding

Marriage is a public service of the Church (*BAS*, p. 526) to be solemnized in the presence of the community. The priest acts on behalf of the Christian community. Previously, marriage could only take place in the church building or, in rare cases, in a hospital or nursing home. General Synod in 2004 said that, while the body of the church is the appropriate place, a marriage may be solemnized in another location if the priest, after consultation with the bishop, is satisfied that "the solemnity and public nature of the occasion will be preserved and that the service will be conducted with dignity in godly and decent order." A wedding could take place during Sunday morning worship, but in practice seldom does.

When you come to the church to plan a wedding, you are asking a community of people if you can join your lives to theirs for this event. You are, in effect, coming into their home. If you are already part of this community, they will share in the joy of your celebration as friends in Christ, and you will already be comfortable with their customs and traditions. If you are new to this community, the priest will outline the customs and traditions that you are asked to observe. These may include guidelines about

- confetti – none in the church, usually! It is terrible to clean up.
- photographs – usually only at certain times in the service and then inconspicuously. Videos are often permitted, again if they can be filmed discreetly.
- music – generally in larger churches you will be given a list of music from which to choose. Music needs to express the Christian dimension of marriage.
- fees – the church has heating, lighting, and cleaning costs. Clergy, musicians, and the caretaker may also need to be paid. Ask what fees are expected; most parishes have a sheet that outlines policies.
- flowers – how many, where may they be placed, what happens to them after the service?
- when can you set up/decorate? Parishes have other events which may limit your time available.

Parishes develop policies about these and other matters, so ask if you can see a copy of their wedding information.

The wedding service

The essential part of the marriage ceremony is the exchange of vows between the bride and groom, and the giving and receiving of a ring. Around that central rite is – of course – a liturgy of prayers, hymns, and readings. One of the authorized liturgies must be used.

Both the *BCP* and the *BAS* services begin with a declaration of the meaning of Christian marriage. We affirm the importance of what we are doing right at the beginning of the wedding service. Marriage is a gift of God and a means of grace by which man and woman become one flesh. The husband and wife are united in love as Christ is united with the Church. Three purposes of marriage are listed:

- the hallowing or blessing of the union between man and woman,
- the procreation of children,
- the mutual comfort and help that the bride and groom give to each other.

Because the priest represents the state as well as the church, he/she calls for a public declaration on the part of the couple that the legal requirements have been met and that there is no impediment to this marriage. The members of the congregation, as witnesses, are asked to affirm this declaration.

Passages from Scripture are read, and prayers offered for the couple.

The actual wedding is the exchange of vows. Each promises to love, honour, and protect the other, and to "forsake all others" and be faithful as long as both shall live. Each then makes a solemn vow "to have and to hold from this day forward; for better, for worse, for richer, for poorer, in sickness and in health, to love and to cherish for the rest of our lives."

Since the revision of *The Book of Common Prayer* in 1959, the wording of the vows has been identical for men and women. The *BCP* includes the traditional statement of "giving away," in which the bride's father or other family member "gives" her to the groom in marriage. The *BAS* instead asks the families of both if they give their blessing to this marriage.

A sacrament, as we have seen earlier, is an outward and visible sign of an inward and spiritual grace. So the outward sign of the sacrament of marriage is the exchange of vows and the giving and receiving of a ring(s) and the joining of hands. The couple themselves actually performs the wedding ceremony. The priest witnesses their vows and pronounces the blessing of the Church upon this marriage.

The service concludes with prayers for this new family. Friends and family members may share in the service by reading the Scripture passages and leading the prayers. The Eucharist may be celebrated. Anglican weddings tend to be a bit longer than weddings of other denominations, particularly if the Eucharist is celebrated. I have vivid memories of city weddings where murmurs were heard from those whose parking meters were running out!

The prayers of the wedding service remind us of the responsibility of the Christian community to provide care and support for new families. The *BAS* service asks us to do all in our power to support and uphold this marriage.

A couple married in a civil ceremony may wish to have their marriage blessed in church. Two forms for such a blessing are found in *Occasional Celebrations* on pages C6 and C14.

Other family services

Thanksgiving for a child

Both the *BCP* and the *BAS* include forms of worship for other family events and occasions.

The *BCP* service of "Thanksgiving after Child-birth" (p. 573) has an alternate title "The Churching of Women." In this rite, which is based on the Jewish rites of purification after childbirth, the new mother comes to the church to thank God for a safe delivery and for the gift of the new child. The Jewish rite, described in Leviticus 12, was based on a belief that a woman who bears a child is unclean and needs purification in order to become part of the community again. In the 1549 Prayer Book, the service was called

"The Order for the Purification of Women." Subsequent revisions of the Prayer Book have moved away from that understanding and the 1959 Prayer Book emphasizes the importance of thanksgiving rather than purification.

The Book of Alternative Services includes a service of "Thanksgiving for the Gift of a Child" with prayers that focus on the child and the family as well as on the mother. Prayers are included for "a child born handicapped." *Occasional Celebrations* includes prayers for use after a miscarriage or the birth of a stillborn child (page D9).

Family prayers

Both the *BAS* and *BCP* include family prayers to use at home. The *BAS* has a series of "Home Prayers," which include graces at meals and prayers for the anniversary of a baptism. The *BCP* has "Forms of Prayer to Be Used in Families" (pp. 728 ff) with outlines for Morning and Evening Prayer.

Family rituals and customs are an important way to teach the Christian faith to all ages. We need to consider how God is active in the whole of our lives and to develop patterns of worship that remind us of God's love and care.

Saying grace, praying together with our children, and developing family customs to celebrate seasons and feast days, can help children understand what it means to belong to the Church. Just as we celebrate birthdays to express our joy at being members of a human family, celebrating the anniversary of Baptism could be a way of expressing our joy at being part of the Christian family.

Customs like lighting the candles on the Advent wreath help families explore the church seasons with children. When our children were young, we used the World Council of Churches prayer cycle before dinner each Sunday, using a prayer from a different country each week. It helped us to remember our brothers and sisters in Christ all over the world. Curriculum materials often contain excellent suggestions for at-home activities, and there is a wealth of material in church bookstores and online for observing the seasons.

Renewal of marriage vows

This custom is becoming more popular in the Anglican Church of Canada. Couples may choose on a special anniversary to renew their marriage vows publicly. A form of liturgy for such an occasion is found in *Occasional Celebrations* on page C2.

At the end of a marriage

Sometimes marriages come to an end and patterns of family life break down. The Church needs to be there with us in our sorrows as well as our joys. *Occasional Celebrations* on page C24 contains prayers which may be used both at home and in church to acknowledge the end of a marriage and to pray for strength and comfort in this difficult time. This resource for worship is not the sort of book that every Anglican home will have. It is a collection of worship materials which may be used as models in putting together services for particular events and occasions. But one copy should be available in your parish as a resource.

15

What happens when we become ill or die?

The *BAS* and the *BCP* both provide direction for visiting the sick, and prayers to be used when ministering to the sick and their families.

Services for the sick and dying

I have been told that the Anglican Church is one of only a few denominations that include services and prayers for healing. These prayers, along with the rites for marriage, burial, and Thanksgiving for the Gift of a Child, are included in *The Book of Alternative Services*. This section, called "Pastoral Offices," is designed to express our belief in God's care for us at significant moments in life's journey. In the prayers for the sick and the dying, we affirm God's care for all creation, and join our prayers with the prayers of the church for healing and wholeness, for a peaceful death, and for comfort for those who mourn.

There are many biblical stories which describe Jesus' care for those who were ill, and his concern for wholeness. The Epistle of James asks the sick to "call for the elders of the church, and let them pray over them, anointing them with oil in the name of the Lord." (James 5:14) Visiting the sick in homes and in hospitals remains an important part of Christian ministry.

From the earliest days of the church, ministry to the sick has been seen as the action of the whole Christian community, and an extension of the church's worship. So we pray for the sick each Sunday in our public worship, and we carry bread and wine to them so that they can share in the Eucharist.

The form of service for the sick in hospital or home may include
• the reading of appropriate passages of Scripture;
• prayers for the sick person;
• the confession and absolution of sin, if the sick person wishes;
• the laying on of hands and anointing with oil with prayers for healing. The oil is blessed by the bishop and is kept in the church. It is often carried in a small container called an "oil stock";
• Holy Communion.

Families may (and should) share in the prayers and the Eucharist. Lay people, when authorized to do so, may pray with the sick, anoint with oil and administer the reserved sacrament. Both the *BAS* and the *BCP* include additional prayers to be used at the time of death (*BAS* page 560, *BCP* page 588).

Healing and pastoral care

Of course, ministry to the sick includes much more than liturgical services. Today in the Anglican Church, lay people are taking responsibility for visiting and pastoral care. Parishes and dioceses are providing training for them. Clergy and chaplains are working to develop skills in this important area of ministry.

In the Anglican Church of Canada, services of prayer for healing are held in many parishes. The Order of St. Luke the Physician is an international association of clergy and lay people who meet to pray for the sick.

The funeral

Funeral customs vary from place to place. Funerals may reflect local customs or the ethnic traditions of the family. So it may be customary to hold a "wake" (in the home, the funeral home, or the church hall) on the evening before the funeral. Every culture has its own traditions, reflecting the universal need to mark death in some way.

As Christians, while we mourn the loss of one who was dear to us, we do so in the light of the resurrection. We believe in a good God who receives us when we die. So Anglican funerals include elements of thanksgiving, both for the life of the person who has died and for God's goodness in receiving us into God's presence.

We need to be angry, to grieve, to raise questions about death. We need to affirm that our sense of loss and our bewilderment is real. But the service reminds us that, in time, we can move through our anger and grieving in the knowledge of Christ's victory over death. However troubled we are over this death, we know that God is good and will give us strength to meet this loss.

The funeral service is a commemoration of the life of the person who has died, and a thanksgiving for all that the person has meant to family and community. And it is also a time to express our loss and grief, to pray for strength and comfort, and to affirm our belief that we along with the dead person share in the new life in Christ.

In many communities, funerals take place in a funeral home with one of the local clergy officiating at the prayers. For the Christian, it is always appropriate to hold a funeral service in the church, within the Christian community where the person was a member.

When my grandmother died, my mother suggested holding the funeral at the funeral home because we are a small family and my grandmother had few friends in the community. We expected only a handful of people at the service, and it was cold February weather. But I was a new graduate from theological college and full of ideas about how things should be done! So we held the funeral in the church. There were only eight people there. But it was an important way for us to mark the death of a woman whose Christian faith coloured her whole life, and it was held within the context of a parish community in which mother, my sister, and I took an active part.

In our town, holding a funeral in church was thought to be quite remarkable. The rector took the opportunity to comment on the appropriateness of our choice the following Sunday!

Both Anglican liturgical books offer a number of forms for funeral services. The service should be planned by the family with the help of the priest or officiant. Elements of the liturgy include the reading of Scripture, the confession of faith (usually the Apostles' Creed), and prayers for the family and for the deceased. It may include the celebration of the Eucharist.

The community meal is always appropriate when the Christian community meets, whether in celebration or in sorrow.

Both books also contain prayers for the "committal," the burial of the body or the disposition of ashes. Cremation is permitted in the Anglican Church. The burial or committal may be separate from the funeral service in time and place.

Sometimes we are responsible for planning a funeral for a family member who did not profess the Christian faith. But, if other family members are active members of a Christian community, a funeral service in the church can be an important way for them to mourn in the company of their parish family, and to express their own Christian hope in God's sustaining love. *Occasional Celebrations* contains a form of service, "Burial of One who Did Not Profess the Christian Faith" (page D2). The prayers are designed to respect the views of the deceased but at the same time to allow the Christian members of the family to express in prayer and worship their own Christian views. The service is appropriate both for those who belong to other world religions and those who profess no faith. The language therefore does not speak of God as Trinity but uses other descriptions of God – Loving God, God of hope, Giver of life, and so on.

Ministry to the families

In the weeks following the death, it is important for us as Christians to continue to support the family as they mourn the one who has died and begin to adjust to life without them. As members of the Christian family, we share each other's joys and sorrows.

Parish churches have many ways to commemorate loved ones. We place flowers in church on the anniversaries of their deaths, to keep their story alive within the parish family. All Souls Day (November 2) is a time when we particularly remember those who have died. The prayers appointed for that day remind us that we are joined with the Communion of Saints, that great group of Christians who have finished their earthly life and with whom we share the hope of resurrection from the dead.

16

Who and what are ministers?

In the last 40 years, the Anglican Church has come to a new understanding of the meaning of ministry. **All** baptized persons are part of the *laos*, the people of God, and **all** are called to bring to others the good news of God's love.

Therefore, **all** Christians are called to ministry. This call is found in the *BCP* Baptism service. Among the duties listed (p. 540) are "walking answerably" to our Christian calling and taking up our cross and following Christ. The obligations of this call are made more explicit in the *BAS*. When we reaffirm our baptismal vows, we promise to proclaim by word and example the good news of God in Christ, to seek and serve Christ in all persons, and to strive for justice and peace among all people (*BAS*, p. 159). When we are baptized, we promise to take on the responsibility of ministry in our own community and situation.

I know a parish, dedicated to All Saints, that lists on its leaflet "Ministers: All baptized members of the congregation." Below that, it then lists the priest, honorary assistant, churchwardens, organist, and all the other particular ministries in the life of that congregation. We are all saints, and we are all ministers.

The ordained ministry

Some people, however, are called to special ministries in the church. They are **ordained** to that work by the laying on of hands and prayers for the gift of the Holy Spirit to carry out their ministry.

The three orders of ordained ministry – bishop, priest, and deacon – have their origins in the New Testament church. Those three names (*episcopos, presbyteros,* and *diakonos*) can be found in the New Testament and in early Christian writings, though it is not always clear what defined the work of each order. However, over the years the Church has developed patterns of work for them.

The **deacon** (from the Greek "servant") is ordained to a ministry of service to others. Some people remain deacons on a permanent basis. Often they are in secular employment. Others are deacons for a period of time and then are ordained to the priesthood. But all the ordained have this ministry of service as the basis of their calling. All priests and bishops are deacons first.

In Canada, deacons have the title "Reverend" and may wear a clerical collar. In some other parts of the Communion, neither is the case. Deacons do not celebrate the Eucharist or pronounce the absolution or blessing, but may read the gospel, preach and baptize when authorized to do so.

During the liturgy (the church service), deacons wear an alb or cassock and surplice, and wear the stole across their left shoulder. If a parish has a full set of Eucharistic vestments, the deacon wears the "dalmatic," a long tunic, over the alb.

The **priest** or presbyter (a Greek word meaning "elder") is ordained following a period as a deacon and is authorized to baptize, to celebrate the Eucharist, to hear confession and to pronounce the absolution. Priests may be placed in charge of parishes (where they are usually called "Rector") or may serve as chaplains to schools, hospitals, prisons or other institutions, or in other forms of ministry. Some priests have secular jobs and work as non-stipendiary clergy (without stipend or salary) in a parish.

Priests have the responsibility for the pastoral care of all those within their jurisdiction. A priest is a member of a diocese, under the authority of a diocesan bishop, and shares with other clergy responsibility for the life of the diocese. Priests wear their stole over both shoulders.

The **bishop** (from the Greek "overseer") has oversight over the church in a particular diocese. There are 30 dioceses in Canada. Some dioceses have assistant bishops as well.

Bishops are elected to their office by representative clergy and laity meeting in synod. They represent the linking of the local church both historically with the apostles and others commissioned by the early church and, in the present day, with other Anglican bishops all around the world.

Bishops are pastors to the clergy and laity. They ordain priests and deacons, and assist in the ordination of other bishops. They appoint clergy to parish and other responsibilities, so a good deal of their time is taken up with personnel work. In the churches of their diocese, they celebrate the rites of Christian Initiation, especially those which affirm the baptismal covenant (Confirmation, reception, and the reaffirmation of baptismal vows). They chair meetings of synod and are responsible for the work of the church in the diocese. Bishops serve on national committees of the Anglican Church of Canada.

They also meet regularly with the other Canadian bishops in what is called "the House of Bishops." This stemmed from a time when General Synod met in two Houses; a House of Bishops and a House of Clergy and Laity. Now both groups meet together at General Synod, every three years. The House of Bishops also meets twice a year, on its own. Provincial Houses of Bishops also meet from time to time.

The ordination of women

In the Anglican Church of Canada, all orders of ministry are open to both men and women. For centuries the ordained ministry of the church was open only to men. Even in the 1960s, when I was a theological student at Trinity College in Toronto, there seemed little thought of ordaining women to the diaconate or priesthood. Women were actively engaged in ministry, as deaconesses and other kinds of professional lay ministry in the church. And of course women had always had a major role in the life of congregations, in fundraising, visiting, and support, even when opportunities for a share in church government were closed to them.

Recent historical studies show us that, in the first centuries of the church's life, women did play major leadership roles and may in fact have been ordained. Somehow, over the centuries, that role was closed to women, though they continued to write and teach theology. We are rediscovering many of the writings of medieval women theologians.

The office of **deaconess** was an ancient one. (The name may be confusing. A deaconess is not simply a female deacon!) References to this office are found in the New Testament and in other writing from the early church. Deaconesses visited the poor and the sick, and had a special ministry to women, particularly in preparing them for Baptism. In 1861, the deaconess order was revived in the Church of England. Women were "set apart" for this ministry by prayer and the laying on of hands.

In 1968, the Lambeth Conference accepted the principle that the diaconate – the order of deacons – was open to both men and women. Those women who had been made deaconesses by laying on of hands were now declared to be deacons, within the order of the diaconate.

The issue of the ordination of women to the priesthood was discussed during much of the 20th century. In 1935, the Archbishop of Canterbury set up a commission on the ministry of women. Its report affirmed the tradition of a priesthood open only to men.

Then in 1944, in wartime, the Bishop of Hong Kong ordained Florence Li Tim-Oi as priest. There was such controversy over her ordination that, after the war, she agreed to stop functioning as a priest. She took up the exercise of her ministry again in 1979, and later settled in Canada.

The 1968 Lambeth Conference reported that it could find no conclusive theological reason for withholding ordination to the priesthood from women, and asked all Provinces to study the issue and to share insights. The Anglican Consultative Council of 1971 agreed that any bishop might ordain women to the priesthood with the approval of his own Province. In 1971, the Canadian House of Bishops agreed to allow the ordination of women to the diaconate, and many deaconesses then became deacons.

The 1973 General Synod accepted the further principle of the ordination of women to the priesthood, and this was affirmed at the General Synod of 1975. The first Canadian women were ordained to the priesthood on November 30, 1976.

A Conscience Clause at that time affirmed that no bishop, priest, deacon, or lay person should be penalized or forced into a position contrary to their conscience as a result of disagreement with this action. Some clergy and lay people were opposed to the ordination of women, largely on the grounds that this step broke with 2,000 years of catholic tradition. Some of these opponents left the Anglican Church to join other churches.

But, in general, the movement for the ordination of women ran relatively smoothly in Canada. I think that this was so for two reasons. There were many women in Canada who had studied theology and who had been actively engaged in professional ministry as lay women. Women had gone to sparsely settled parts of the country to visit, teach, and run parishes. Women workers had served in inner city congregations teaching, doing social work, and assisting with parish programs. So among the first to be ordained were many who had years of experience in ministry and who were already well-respected for their gifts.

A second factor, I think, is the orderly way in which the ordination came about. All the legal steps were followed, as the discussion took place at every level of the church's life. By contrast, in the United States an "illegal" ordination of 11 women took place in Philadelphia before the legislation could be passed in the General Convention (their national governing body, like our General Synod). This action caused a good deal of controversy and I think gave the ordination of women rougher passage into the life of that church.

Women are not ordained in all Provinces of the Anglican Communion. The Church of England only ordained women to the priesthood in 1994, almost 20 years after women were first ordained in Canada.

After acceptance of the ordination of women became widespread in Canada, the conscience clause was rescinded in 1986, and today women are ordained in every diocese of the Canadian church. Women clergy are now rectors of rural and urban parishes, chaplains, theologians and teachers, archdeacons and canons and regional deans, members of diocesan and national committees, and members of General Synod.

The process of admitting women to all three orders of ministry was completed in 1994, when the first woman bishop in Canada was ordained. The Rt. Rev. Victoria Matthews was first an Area Bishop in the Diocese of Toronto, and then Bishop of Edmonton. She is now the Bishop of Christchurch, New Zealand. Since that time a number of other women have been ordained as bishops, bringing their many gifts to the life of the Canadian church. They have taken their place at Lambeth Conferences when bishops gather from all over the Anglican Communion.

Ordinations

The Ordinal (or ordination rite) in the *BCP* speaks of "making" deacons, "ordaining" priests, and "consecrating" bishops. The *BAS* uses the same terminology for all three orders, describing the service as "the ordination" of the bishop, priest, or deacon and the central act of laying on of hands with prayer as "the consecration" of the bishop, priest, or deacon. You will find the ordination services on pages 637 to 667 in the *BCP*, and pages 632 to 666 in the *BAS*.

Ordinations follow a similar pattern: prayers and Scripture readings, the examination of the candidate and the swearing of the required oaths, the laying on of hands by the bishop with prayer for the gift of the Holy Spirit for this ministry, and the presentation of symbols of office. In most cases, the service concludes with the celebration of the Eucharist.

Training

Clergy generally train for ministry at a theological college. There are a number of these in Canada. Some are denominational; others are ecumenical, combining students and faculty of several denominations and sharing in the worship and traditions of each group. There are also a number of other training institutions that offer programs with a specific focus, such as aboriginal or regional concerns, or training for lay ministry.

Students preparing for ordination must go before a regional board called the Advisory Committee on Postulants for Ordination (ACPO). This committee of clergy and lay people assesses the suitability of the candidate for training and ordination, and makes recommendations to the colleges and the bishops. The *BCP* lists minimum age requirements for those to be ordained; deacons must be 23 years of age, priests 24, and bishops 30.

Lay people also may study at theological colleges and other training centres. Many lay people have a deep desire to explore the Scriptures, learn the tradition and history of their church, and examine ethical issues in the light of the gospel. I believe that it is important to have theologically-trained lay people in the church helping us reflect on theological issues, teaching faith to others, and enriching the life of the congregation and diocese with their insights.

Theology is too important to be left merely to the clergy! I believe that clergy need to see themselves as teachers equipping lay people for their own ministry in the church and in the world.

What people wear

Clergy, and sometimes lay assistants such as choir members and servers, wear special robes for worship. These robes derive from the ordinary street dress of gentlemen of the early centuries, because Christians fearing persecution tried to dress just like other people. But by the fourth century, when Christianity became a legal religion recognized by the state, certain garments were worn only for religious rites; we have retained many of them with very little change.

- **Alb:** from "albus" (white). A long white robe belted with a girdle or cincture (usually a rope or cord). At one time, the alb was worn only under the chasuble. Now it is common for Anglican priests to wear only a cassock-alb with the stole. Albs may be worn by servers or other assistants.

- **Chasuble:** a poncho-like garment in the liturgical colour of the season. The principal Eucharistic vestment, although some clergy prefer to wear cassock and surplice.

- **Stole:** a narrow strip of material in the colour of the season. It probably represents the towel with which Jesus girded himself as he washed the disciples' feet. Priests and bishops wear the stole around the neck and hanging down on both sides. Deacons wear the stole over the left shoulder.

- **Cassock and Surplice:** "choir dress," worn for the choir offices of Morning and Evening Prayer (which were traditionally sung). The cassock is a long black robe (white in tropical countries) that was worn by clergy as street dress at one time. Choir members and servers also wear cassocks of any colour. Bishops wear purple cassocks. Sometimes the cassock is worn with a small shoulder cape. The surplice is a shorter white robe worn over the cassock. Generally it has wide sleeves. The name comes from the term *superpellicium* or something worn over a fur-lined cassock. Today in well-heated Canadian churches, clergy wear cassock and surplice but never with fur lining! Cassock and surplice may also be worn by choir members and servers.

- **Scarf:** a strip of black material worn around the neck for the choir offices. It is sometimes called a "preaching scarf" or "tippet." The scarf probably derives from the academic hood. Clergy sometimes wear their academic hoods for Morning and Evening Prayer.

- Bishops have their own distinctive vestments. The traditional colour associated with Anglican bishops is purple, so bishops generally wear purple shirts and purple cassocks.

- **Ring:** a sign of the bond between the bishop and the diocese. Sometimes the episcopal ring has a purple stone, generally an amethyst. The Greek word for amethyst means "not drunk" and refers to the description of the apostles at Pentecost (Acts 2:15). The ring may include the crest of the diocese, which may be used to imprint the bishop's seal on letters and official documents.

- **Pectoral Cross:** Bishops also wear a pectoral cross ("pectoral" meaning worn on the chest). A bishop carries a **crozier** or pastoral staff, usually in the form of a shepherd's crook, as a sign of authority and jurisdiction in the diocese.

- **Cope:** a long cape fastened with a clasp at the front. The clasp is usually of precious material and elaborately decorated. Other clergy may also wear the cope in processions.

- **Mitre:** a tall divided hat worn by bishops. It is generally of precious material to match the cope. Its shape symbolizes the tongues of flame that descended upon the apostles at Pentecost. The two tabs that fall from the back of the mitre are called "lappets."

- **Rochet:** a long white surplice worn by bishops over the purple cassock, with full sleeves and optional ruffles at the wrists, worn for non-Eucharistic worship. The ruffles are the remains of the Elizabethan frill once worn by all clergy.

- **Chimere:** a sleeveless gown, generally scarlet but may also be black. It is similar to the doctoral gown.

Clergy titles

Clergy use the title "The Reverend" as a sign of office. Strictly speaking, the title is an adjective and not a direct title of address. So it is correct to say "The Reverend Mr. Smith" or "The Reverend Dorothy Smith," but not "Reverend Smith." It is a good idea to ask clergy what they prefer to be called. Very often today clergy prefer simply to be called by their Christian names. But using Mr., Mrs., or Ms in formal situations is never wrong.

Bishops may be addressed simply as "Bishop Smith." In informal situations, many bishops like to be called by their Christian names. Be sure to ask if you are in any doubt. There are old historical titles – "My Lord" for bishops, and "Your Grace" for Archbishops – but these are now used less frequently.

An **Archbishop** (The Most Reverend) is the chief bishop of an ecclesiastical province. In Canada, there are 4 provinces – Canada, Ontario, Rupert's Land, and British Columbia and Yukon. Each has an Archbishop with responsibilities for the oversight of the province and of provincial synod. The Archbishop of a province is called a **Metropolitan**.

The **Primate** is the chief bishop of the Anglican Church of Canada. He is an Archbishop but without territory. His office is at Church House, he chairs General Synod and the House of Bishops, visits all parts of our church, and represents our church at national, international and ecumenical events.

A **Bishop** (The Right Reverend) has the responsibility of the oversight of all the ministry of the church in a particular area called a **diocese**. A diocese may also have a **coadjutor** bishop (one who will succeed the retiring diocesan bishop) and a **suffragan**, **area** or **assistant** bishop (one who does not automatically succeed).

The bishop delegates responsibility for particular locations, or parishes, to certain clergy. A priest to whom the bishop designates care for a parish is usually called a **Rector**, though sometimes called "the incumbent" or "the vicar."

The **Dean** (The Very Reverend) is generally rector of the Cathedral. The Cathedral has a special role in the diocese. It is the location of the bishop's "cathedra" or chair, a symbol of the bishop's role as chief pastor of the diocese. The cathedral is often the setting for special diocesan events and gatherings and is, in some sense, the "mother church" of the diocese. The Dean is a senior priest in the diocese, and frequently serves as the bishop's deputy or commissary in administrative matters if the bishop is ill or away from the diocese.

An **Archdeacon** (The Venerable) is a priest with certain administrative responsibilities. Archdeacons assist the bishop in the day-to-day running of the diocese. Some archdeacons are parish priests and have responsibilities for geographical areas of the diocese. They respond to the needs of parishes and clergy, and inspect church property to see that it is maintained. Some archdeacons work in the synod office as administrators.

Rural/Regional Deans are clergy with some responsibilities for oversight within their deanery, a smaller area of the diocese. Regional deans call area clergy together for meetings. Sometimes the archdeacons and regional deans meet to advise and assist the bishop. At one time these persons were called "Rural Deans" even though they might live and work downtown in a major city! The old name stems from a much earlier time when the Church of England was a largely rural church. The new name reflects more accurately the reality of both rural and urban life.

Canon is an honorary title given to a priest or lay person in recognition of their dedicated service to the church. Canons have special seats in the cathedral and, in some cases, the canons along with the Dean form a "chapter" of clergy which governs the life of the cathedral.

In church processions, the person who walks last has the most authority. In each diocese, for example, the bishop walks last in the procession. At the opening of General Synod, the Primate comes at the end of the procession. When the Archbishop of Canterbury visits us in Canada, he would precede the Primate or the diocesan bishop.

The laity

Most church members are not ordained to special ministries. In recent years we have caught a new vision of the ministry of all the people of God, and lay people are involved in many varied roles both in the life of the congregation and in the world outside the church building. There are many lay people who work in professional lay ministries in education and training, in administration, in outreach and work for social justice, in pastoral care and service. Threshold Ministries (formerly the Church Army) is a society of lay men and women who are trained for ministries of evangelism, teaching, and social service.

The Anglican Church has **religious orders** of men and women who live in community and dedicate their lives to ministries of prayer, education, and hospitality. Canadian orders for women include the Sisters of St. John the Divine, the Sisters of the Church, and the Society of Our Lady St. Mary. Orders for men include the Order of the Holy Cross, and the Society of St. John the Evangelist. Religious orders were founded as part of a lay movement in the church. Today some monks and nuns are ordained priests, but most are lay people.

17

How is our Church organized?

The symbol of the Anglican Communion is the **Compass Rose** (sometimes spelled Compasrose) inscribed with the Greek, "The truth shall make you free."

Like all organizations, the Anglican Church has developed structures to enable it to do its work. These operate at many levels, from local to international.

Congregation and parish

The smallest structural unit is the **congregation**. Groups of Anglicans gather together in one place for weekly worship, for community and support, for mission and outreach. (Roman Catholics use this word in a different way, to refer to a religious order or sometimes to executive departments within the structure of the Curia or central administration in Rome.)

Each congregation elects representatives to the **vestry** or **council,** its governing body. The vestry/parish council takes responsibility for looking after the congregation's buildings, finances, and programs. Each congregation has wardens, who together with the incumbent have the legal responsibility for the parish. Generally one warden is chosen by the people, and is called the People's Warden. The Rector's Warden is appointed by the rector or incumbent. The regulations about these forms of government are set out in diocesan canons.

An individual congregation may be a **parish** (or self-governing unit) by itself. Or it may join with other congregations to form a parish. The parish council for a multi-point parish includes lay representatives from each congregation and is responsible for decisions affecting the whole parish. The parish annual meeting allows all parishioners to share in decision-making.

In England, the Church of England is an established church. Therefore, Church of England parishes must take responsibility for every person who lives within the parish boundaries, whether they are Anglicans or not. So the parish priest takes baptisms, weddings, and funerals for people living within parish boundaries even if they do not attend church. In Canada, parish membership is less easily defined. Anglicans become members of a parish simply by attending on a regular basis. Diocesan canons or laws define who may vote at the annual meeting. These canons may stipulate that a person must be a certain age or must have attended services regularly for a period of time.

The bishop is the chief pastor in the diocese. But because the bishop cannot be everywhere at once, a priest is appointed by the bishop as rector or incumbent of the parish. In the induction service, the service at which the ministry of a new incumbent is celebrated, the bishop hands over to the new incumbent the responsibility for the oversight of pastoral ministry in this particular place. "Let all these be signs of the ministry which is mine and yours, and is shared by all the people of God" (*Occasional Celebrations*, page E9). "Accept this charge which is mine and thine" (*BCP*, p. 671).

Traditionally, Anglican parishes have employed seminary-trained stipendiary clergy; clergy whose salary and expenses are paid by the parish from its revenues of offerings, rentals, and endowments. Now in some places, it is increasingly difficult for parishes to raise these funds. Declining numbers, rural depopulation, and financial recession have strained parish budgets. Dioceses are experiencing financial difficulties and are increasingly unable to supply additional funds to parishes. So dioceses and parishes are looking at new ways to provide ministry in these situations. Sometimes part-time or semi-retired clergy are able to serve in a particular place. Sometimes parishes are able to work more closely with Christians of other denominations in their area.

A number of parishes are developing local ministry teams made up of lay people willing to take responsibility for areas of ministry previously done only by the clergy. Through our renewed understanding of the meaning of Baptism, we have come to realize that all baptized are called to ministry in the community in which they live. Many kinds of ministry can be shared by lay people: visiting in homes and hospitals, education, leading in worship, financial matters, social action.

So dioceses are setting up training schemes to give lay people the skills for ministry they need, and in some places are exploring the possibility of ordaining people from the congregation as deacons or priests. A number of parishes are governed by **lay ministry teams**, who together agree to take on many of the responsibilities that the parish priest once had.

The deanery

A group of parishes in a geographical area forms a deanery. Parish representatives meet from time to time for education, planning, and support. The deanery chooses one of its number, usually one of the clergy, to serve for a period of time as Regional Dean coordinating and chairing deanery gatherings.

The archdeaconry

Dioceses are also generally divided into two, three, or more larger groupings known as Archdeaconries. The bishop appoints an Archdeacon to certain administrative responsibilities. The archdeacons assist the bishop in the day-to-day running of the diocese, and meet with the bishop from time to time to give advice and share in making decisions. Some archdeacons are parish priests and have responsibilities for a particular geographical area of the diocese. Some archdeacons work in the synod office as administrators.

The diocese

The diocese is a geographical area under the leadership of the diocesan bishop. There are 30 dioceses in Canada. Every parish at its annual meeting elects representatives to the diocesan **synod**, a "parliament" which meets from time to time to discuss the concerns of the church in the area and to make decisions affecting its life. Synod is made up of both clergy and lay members. Synod is generally chaired by the bishop. The "Bishop's Charge" or address to synod outlines the bishop's vision and hopes for the diocese as well as recounting some of the history of the diocese since synod last met.

Synod agrees upon a budget for diocesan work. Funds come from the parishes on an apportionment basis. Each parish, on the basis of the number of members and the amount of its annual budget, contributes a share of its funds for work in the diocese. Dioceses work out a formula for each parish to contribute its fair share to diocesan work. The money pays for the salary and expenses of the bishop and other diocesan staff, and for the program work of the diocese. A portion of diocesan funds is sent on to the national church as the diocese's share of that work.

Synod sets up committees of clergy and laity to do the work of ministry in the diocese in such areas as finance, education, doctrine and worship, evangelism, social action, long-range planning, mission, and ministry. The diocesan council or executive is elected to make decisions between synods. The chancellor is an appointed official of the diocese, a lawyer who advises the diocese on legal matters as well as seeing that the regulations as set down in the canons (laws of the diocese) are observed.

Dioceses also employ staff to work from the synod office developing programs and administering the diocese.

The ecclesiastical province

The province is a group of dioceses covering a larger area and under the leadership of an archbishop, also called a Metropolitan. (In this book, I use a capital "P" to designate the national church as Province [see below], and a lower-case "p" to describe Canada's internal provinces.) Dioceses send representatives to provincial synod to discuss issues of common concern. One area of particular concern to provinces is training for ministry.

There are four ecclesiastical provinces in Canada. Here are the dioceses of each province, listed alphabetically.

Province of British Columbia and Yukon	Province of Ontario
Anglican Parishes of the Central Interior (formerly Cariboo)	Algoma
British Columbia	Huron
Caledonia	Moosonee
Kootenay	Niagara
New Westminster	Ontario
Yukon	Ottawa
	Toronto

Province of Rupert's Land	Province of Canada
Athabasca	Central Newfoundland
Arctic	Eastern Newfoundland and Labrador
Brandon	Fredericton
Calgary	Montreal
Edmonton	Nova Scotia
Keewatin	Quebec
Qu'Appelle	Western Newfoundland
Rupert's Land	
Saskatchewan	
Saskatoon	

The national church

In many cases, the national church is called a Province. The Anglican Church of Canada is a Province, as is the Church of England. Each national Province is independent, making its own laws and governing its own life. Each Province has its own senior bishop, sometimes called Archbishop, Primate or Presiding Bishop, who chairs the church's governing body. Each Province of the Communion makes the laws or canons that govern its life. So some Provinces have made a decision to ordain women to the priesthood and the episcopate; some have decided not to. Some Provinces of the Communion permit the remarriage of divorced persons whose former spouse is still living; some do not. Each Province is free to make its own decisions, not merely in matters of cultural custom, but also in matters of profound theological significance. See Chapter 20 for more information on making decisions as a Communion.

The Anglican Church of Canada is under the leadership of the Primate, an Archbishop and the chief pastor of the national church. Dioceses send bishops, priests, and lay people to General Synod, which meets every three years to make decisions about national church life. In between synods, decisions are made by the Council of General Synod, which meets twice a year and includes representatives from the dioceses. The House of Bishops also meets twice a year.

The work of the Canadian church is carried on through national staff at Church House, our national headquarters in Toronto, and through national committees made up of bishops, priests, and lay people. These committees are concerned with such matters as world mission and overseas partnerships, faith, worship and ministry, program, administration and finance, organization, pensions, and so on.

These committees and structures change from time to time to respond to the needs of the church and the world. The church publishes a monthly newspaper, *The Anglican Journal*, which is sent to every home on parish mailing lists. The work of relief and development (both overseas and in Canada) is carried on through the Primate's World Relief and Development Fund, which collects and distributes money. The website of the Anglican Church of Canada gives more information about this work.

The international church

The Anglican Communion has 80 million members worldwide. It is a family of 44 regional and national member churches. There are 34 Provinces, four united churches (the churches of North India, South India, Pakistan, and Bangladesh), and six regional churches. Most branches of the Communion are called "Anglican," reminding us of our historical roots in the Church of England. Some churches are called Episcopal ("having bishops") or Episcopalian – for example, in the United States and Scotland, countries where the Church of England connection was not particularly an asset.

As members of a family of churches, we join from time to time with other Anglicans around the world to share ideas and to learn from each other.

The Lambeth Conference

Periodically, the bishops from all the member churches of the Anglican Communion meet in Canterbury, the home of the Church of England. They were first called by the Archbishop of Canterbury to meet in 1867, Canada's Confederation year, at the request of Canadian bishops.

The Lambeth Conference is now held every ten years. The most recent conference was held in 2008 and included over 800 bishops. Spouses attended a parallel gathering, at the invitation of the wife of the Archbishop.

The conference has no legislative power, but its statements carry a great deal of weight. Many of its statements on social issues have influenced church policy in the national churches. One landmark statement was that of Lambeth 1930 which stated that the use of artificial means of birth control was acceptable for Anglicans. Every diocese in the world has a share in these discussions, so this group is very important in the life of our church.

The **Primates** (or chief bishops) of the Provinces meet from time to time. The Primates' meeting was established in 1978 as an opportunity for "leisurely thought, prayer, and deep consultation."

The Anglican Consultative Council

This is a gathering of bishops, priests, and lay people representing the Provinces of the international Anglican Communion. They meet every three years to reflect on mission, ecumenism, doctrine, and social justice issues.

It is the only international body where priests and lay people take part in discussion alongside the bishops. The Anglican Church of Canada has three members: a bishop, a priest, and a lay person. I was the lay member for Canada for a term of three meetings of the Council (about seven years) during the 1980s. During that time, the Council met in England, Nigeria and Singapore, with executive meetings in England and Scotland. We also attended the 1988 Lambeth Conference, with voice but not vote. It was a great privilege to be able to participate in the life of the Church in this way. I had the opportunity to meet Anglicans from all over the world, to worship in churches in many different cultures, and to take part in interesting and challenging discussions on a variety of issues.

Through the ACC we also participate in a number of ecumenical dialogues such as those described in Chapter 9, and work with other Anglican Provinces on inter-Anglican commissions which look at doctrine, worship, mission, families, and other issues from time to time.

All of these gatherings are important ways of strengthening the life of the Anglican family. We have much in common with our Anglican sisters and brothers, and we need to foster these opportunities to learn from one another.

Funding

How do we fund our participation in all these groups? The answer is simple: from our offerings on the collection plate each week and at other special times. The money we give in the parish begins a journey that takes part of it all over the world. Our parish sends its apportionment to the diocese. The diocese then sends a part of that money on to the national church for the work it does on our behalf. The Anglican Church of Canada sends our share of the funds required to support the international Anglican gatherings and program. So financial cutbacks in the parish have an effect all the way along the line. If we cannot meet our financial obligations in the diocese, then national and international work is also impacted.

18

How do indigenous Anglicans take part in the life of the church?

Some history

The Anglican Church of Canada always had First Nations members; early clergy ministered to Native peoples as well as the British settlers. In 1753 the Rev. Thomas Wood began his work as a missionary to the Mi'kmaq people.

Some of the oldest Anglican parishes in Canada are Native congregations. In central Canada, some significant contacts were made with the Mohawk nation, work that was strengthened during the American Revolution when Native people loyal to the crown came north to Canadian territory.

In the West, members of the Church Missionary Society developed work with the aboriginal people. Very early in this work, the Anglican Church saw the need to train Native leaders. In 1850, Henry Budd was the first Canadian Native priest to be ordained. His example has been followed by many since then, and the Anglican Church has produced a long line of gifted male and female indigenous priests.. In 1989 Charles Arthurson became the first Native bishop in Canada. Since then he has been joined in that order by seven First Nations, Inuit, and Metis people. There are at present 130 indigenous Anglican priests in Canada. About 225 congregations are entirely or almost entirely indigenous in membership. You can learn more by checking the Anglican Church of Canada website.

In some parts of Canada, the Christian denominations agreed among themselves to divide up the work. (Native people were not consulted.)

Some areas were administered by Anglicans, some by Roman Catholics, Methodist, or Presbyterian missions. The early work among Inuit and Indian people in the Arctic was largely done by Anglican missionaries, and most Christian Inuit today are Anglican.

Residential schools

When the Canadian government made treaties with various groups of aboriginal peoples, tracts of land were set aside for their use in perpetuity. Missionaries assisted the aboriginal people to build churches and schools on the reserves, and encouraged the development of agriculture. As part of the treaty obligation to provide education for the indigenous peoples, the government also established a system of residential schools across the country and asked the churches to administer them. About 80 schools were set up, and the Anglican Church was responsible for about 20. The number of the schools varied from the 1880s until 1969 as new schools were built and old ones closed.

We are learning now of the negative effects of the residential school system imposed on Native people, and the abusive behaviour of a few people within that system. In 1993, the Primate, the Most Rev. Michael Peers, made a formal apology to Native people on behalf of the Anglican Church for harms which had been done. This apology, and the apology made by the federal government on whose behalf the churches ran the schools, have been important steps in the work of reconciliation with aboriginal Anglicans.

The effects of residential schools were not all bad. Many present-day leaders of Native communities received their early education in residential schools, and many speak with thankfulness of the dedicated teachers and administrators who worked there.

In 2008, the Truth and Reconciliation Commission was created as part of the Indian Residential School Settlement Agreement, the largest settlement agreement in Canadian history. This agreement was supported by the Government of Canada, the Assembly of First Nations, all of the Church entities that operated residential schools, and other parties to the settlement agreement. The Commission has invited former students and staff to tell their stories, to describe in their own words their experiences at residential schools. The commissioners have held national and community events, and received submissions from individuals, in order to allow the widest possible number to tell their stories. The Anglican Church of Canada, committed to healing and reconciliation, has supported the work of this Commission and has shared archival material regarding the schools.

A voice in the life of the church

In 1967, the Anglican Church of Canada commissioned sociologist Charles Hendry to study the relationship between the Anglican Church and aboriginal people. His 1969 report *Beyond Traplines* called on the church to develop a new partnership with aboriginal peoples.

In succeeding years, steps were taken to give aboriginal Anglicans a greater voice in the life of the church. The hiring of national staff and the forming of councils with a voice at the National Executive Council (now Council of General Synod) have given aboriginal people a stronger voice in the church's decision-making structure. In 1995, the name of the Council for Native Ministries was changed to the Anglican Council of Indigenous Peoples. Members of the Anglican Council of Indigenous Peoples (ACIP) participate in the Anglican Indigenous Network of the Anglican Communion.

In 1988, the first Native Convocation was held in Fort Qu'Appelle, Saskatchewan, with representation from across Canada. Since that time five other convocations, now known as the Anglican Indigenous Sacred Circle, have been held. In 2005, those present at the Sacred Circle in Pinawa, Manitoba, sent a request to the appropriate councils of the Anglican Church of Canada to "adopt a process for the election of subsequent National Indigenous bishops by a Sacred Circle representative of all Canadian Indigenous Anglicans, and to empower the National Indigenous Bishop with episcopal and pastoral responsibilities, as well as full authority and jurisdiction for aboriginal communities across Canada." In 2007, Bishop Mark MacDonald became pastoral leader to Canadian Indigenous Anglicans.

A new partnership

Today, the Anglican Church is committed to working with aboriginal clergy and lay people through ACIP and other groups. In April 1994, representatives of the indigenous people of the Anglican Church of Canada pledged themselves to a covenant, expressed in these words:

> *Under the guidance of God's spirit we agree to do all we can to call our people into unity in a new, self-determining community within the Anglican Church of Canada. To this end, we extend the hand of partnership to all those who will help us build a truly Anglican indigenous Church in Canada.*

The National Executive Council in 1994 welcomed the invitation of the indigenous peoples and pledged its support and willingness to enter into dialogue. The New Agape document speaks of the importance of healing and reconciliation, the encouraging of cross-cultural encounters as well as work to establish a self-determining Anglican Indigenous Community and the church's continued work in support of justice for Indigenous peoples.

This process is unfolding. It is a journey together in faith into new structures and relationships. A statement of the Anglican Council of Indigenous Peoples, found on the Anglican Church of Canada website, acknowledges the pain and hardship caused for many by the residential school experience, but goes on to say,

> *Yet, there have been times, too, when the churches have been our best support in the Canadian society – against those who coveted our land, who would see the death of our language and culture... We are in this together, and we will continue to journey together... guided by the Holy Spirit...seeking the healing of our relationships and ways of being who we are... both fully Christian and fully Aboriginal.*

19

How do Anglicans deal with conflict within the church?

Anglicanism has always been characterized by a diversity of theological emphases, canons, and customs. For centuries we have held within one family conservatives and liberals, catholics, evangelicals, and charismatics. Balancing it all has not been easy. At some times, certain ways of expressing the Christian faith have been more prominent than others. Yet our history shows that we tend to return to a tolerant middle road.

In recent times, the Anglican Church of Canada and the Anglican Communion worldwide have struggled with a number of issues (human sexuality, the interpretation of scripture, the exercise of authority in the life of the Anglican Communion, and the tension between unity and uniformity) that have put strains on the "bonds of affection" that hold the Anglican family together.

A look at history reminds us that dealing with controversy is not peculiar to our own era. The Christian Church has had to deal with a diversity of views as it struggles to understand and describe God and God's relationship with humankind. The historic creeds were composed in response to varied theological opinion about the nature of God the Trinity. Christians debated theology in the marketplace and came to blows in the streets as they advanced differing views of how to describe God. The history of the Church is, in part, the story of how differences were expressed and how the Church divided into smaller groups, each expressing a particular way of experiencing the life of faith. An Internet search reveals an astonishing number of groups today who call themselves Christian. And the Anglican Church is no exception. A look at the website www.anglicansonline.org lists 136 different "continuing Anglican" groups, although they are not in communion with the See of Canterbury.

Schism is one way to deal with problem of diversity. But a look at history might help us examine other ways in which Anglicans have handled differences of opinion and belief.

Synodical decision-making

Early on in the British Isles, Christians faced different practices in regard to the date of Easter. The Celtic Church had one way of calculating the date. The Roman Church had another. Northern kingdoms tended to support the Celtic dating, whereas southern kingdoms supported the method used on the Continent. The Venerable Bede, in his history of church and people, tells us that the king of Northumbria was celebrating Easter while his wife, raised in Kent, was observing Palm Sunday.

While the presenting issue had to do with customs and traditions, behind it was the issue of authority. Who had the authority to say which custom should prevail in a certain area? What sources in Scripture or tradition could be invoked in support of a particular custom?

A synod of clergy and monks that brought together leading church figures from many parts of Britain was held in 664 at the monastery of Whitby. In the end, the king made the decision to side with Rome. This is not, of course, synodical decision-making as we have come to understand it – that is, a council of bishops, clergy, and laity making decisions to govern the life of the community. But it is an important example of the practice of bringing together all the stakeholders to take counsel about how to resolve divisive issues.

Compromise

In Chapter 2, I described some of the turmoil of the 16th-century Reformation. The greatest wish of Elizabeth I was to ensure stability following the tumultuous reigns of Henry VIII, Edward VI, and Mary. Given that political turmoil, what kind of church could best be established in England? Within Elizabeth's realm, religious practices ranged from traditional liturgies to practices influenced by the Calvinist and Lutheran reforms in Europe. Elizabeth's solution was a compromise. Early in her reign, she established guidelines for the worship, governance, and theology of the church that balanced tradition and Catholic sacramental structure with the needs for reform and Protestant theological understandings. The 1559 Prayer Book included both Catholic and reformed understandings of the Eucharist. Liturgies left room for broad interpretation and a variety of theological beliefs and customs. The theological approach was understood as a balance between Scripture, tradition, and reason. The results of this Elizabethan Settlement set the tone for Anglicanism over centuries. Ours is a church that tolerates a variety of liturgical traditions and customs. Our strength lies in our ability to hold together in one family a diversity of expressions.

Holding the balance

The English Civil War of the mid-1600s, fought between monarchists and republicans, between Anglicans and more radical Protestants, highlighted the difficulties of trying to enforce narrow conformity. The Church of England was re-established after the Civil War, but with a limited tolerance for other religious groups. Balancing diversity of views seemed the best solution for church and people.

Two revival movements with very different theological backgrounds – the Evangelical movement (18th century) and the Anglo-Catholic revival (19th century) – brought a reawakening of theological understanding and personal spirituality. Each in its own way enriched the life of the church and had concern for the urban poor and overseas missions. These two streams continue today to some extent, and we have developed a way of living with them and appreciating our differences as we work for the common good.

Welcoming conflict

In the late 19th and early 20th centuries, the rapid advance in scientific understanding raised questions. How could the writings of Charles Darwin be reconciled with the book of Genesis? What did new discoveries about the nature of the universe say about the Church's centuries-old teachings? Did the new science make the scriptures untrue? Could a person embrace the findings of the new science and still remain a Christian? Anglican scholars such as Bishop Charles Gore welcomed the debate, and writings such as *Lux Mundi* reaffirmed that the church welcomes and receives new knowledge, using human reason under the guidance of the Holy Spirit. Anglicans have always placed a high value on scholarship and study, and dealing with diversity in the church may certainly include tackling issues head-on and exploring the variety of arguments for and against a particular position.

Including all

The later 20th century was preoccupied with questions of equality. Are all people equally members of the church? Are women to be included as fully as men in all levels of church life, including the ordained ministry? What is the place of gay and lesbian people in the life of the church? How can aboriginal people celebrate their heritage and traditions while remaining part of the Anglican Church of Canada?

These issues are still under discussion today: the authority of scripture, the changing roles of men and women in society, changing understandings of human sexuality, the affirmation of the rights, including marriage, of gays and lesbians in Canada, issues of power and authority. How should decisions be made? Should decisions be postponed until all parts of the church are agreed? While the speed of decision-making has been frustrating to many, our custom is to move through the synodical process to involve representatives of all parts of the country, of all interest groups, in making decisions the church can live with.

Listening to each other

In the 21st century, the central question is: How can we live together as a family of 44 autonomous Provinces and churches? Modern communications have made us much more aware of developments in other parts of the Anglican Communion. Because each Province is free to make its own decisions, there is a variety of practice, particularly in regard to the role of women in the ministries of the church. Recent decisions in Canada and the United States to make the church more inclusive of gay and lesbian people have sparked reactions from other parts of the world. Behind these discussions are important issues: the authority of Scripture, the roles of men and women in different societies, the legal status of homosexuals in different cultures, the exercise of power and authority in a diocese and in the life of the Communion, the legacy of colonialism, and the question of dispersed or centralized authority in the Anglican Communion.

Recent developments in the life of the Communion (see Chapter 20) seem to indicate greater centralization in the international structures of the Anglican Communion. At the same time, Provinces are affirming their canonical right to make decisions about the life of the church in their own Province. The Primates (or chief bishops) have committed themselves to a "listening process" involving all sides in the debate. In exploring areas of division, it is imperative that all sides take time to listen to the other to discern how the voice of the Holy Spirit is speaking through the experience of our sisters and brothers in the faith.

Learning from history

Over six centuries, we have been able to hold together in one family Christians with a variety of approaches to theology and understandings of scripture. The question of the authority of scripture is one that has concerned Anglicans from earliest times. When we have tried to force a narrow conformity, such as in the 17th century, it has not been a success. Can we produce something like the Elizabethan Settlement that would allow us to exist together, as a family but without uniformity?

Making difficult decisions

How might we make decisions in times of controversy?

We need to recognize that making difficult decisions takes time. As Anglicans we are committed to a synodical process, making decisions by calling together representatives of all parts of the church to share information, to discuss implications, to debate possible solutions, and to try and arrive at a solution that the majority can live with. Diocesan synods meet at most once a year. General Synod meets every three years. Therefore it takes some time for issues to be debated and decisions reached.

We need to hear and respect differing views, recognizing that historically we are a church that has held together a variety of theological viewpoints and emphases. We should not try to force a more narrow conformity than has been our custom. Anglicanism is more like a conversation or a dialogue than a set of doctrines precisely defined. We would do well to remember our history, and the different ways in which decisions have been reached, and allow some latitude for parts of the communion to make decisions that meet the needs of their people.

We need to see if we can agree on a larger principle that underlies both sides of the argument. Accepting such a principle (for example, the idea that God's reign includes all peoples and races) might allow us to live together in one family, while permitting some diversity of practice. The Lambeth Conference of 1968 defined "comprehensiveness" as implying "a willingness to allow liberty of interpretation, with a certain slowness in arresting or restraining exploratory thinking." We should not be too quick to force uniformity on a church that has never been uniform in its practice.

20

How do we live as part of a family of churches?

Being part of a family is not easy. Tensions arise as a result of our different histories and cultures. In Chapter 1, we looked at the spread of Anglicanism in the 19th century as the British Empire expanded throughout the world, and Chapter 17 describes the structures that have developed in order to allow us to live together in the family of churches that we call the Anglican Communion. Each Province of the Communion is an independent body that governs its own life. Today our rapid means of travel and electronic communication systems mean that news of events in one Province travels quickly to all parts of the Anglican Communion. There can be an immediate response, either of approval or disapproval, to any action taken by a member Province. With the advent of social media, discussions take place in the public forum; blogs express one viewpoint or another, and like-minded people form networks within one Province or across the Communion.

A current debate in the church has to do with the authority of Provinces to make decisions with regard to issues around human sexuality. At issue are matters such as the authority and interpretation of Scripture, how much diversity of practice should be permitted, and the authority of the councils of the church (the Lambeth Conference, the Anglican Consultative Council, and the Primates' Meeting) in determining policy for individual Provinces. The councils of the Communion (the Anglican Consultative Council and the Lambeth Conference) have traditionally been permissive rather than legislative. For example, the councils allowed some Provinces to proceed with the ordination of women while not requiring others to do so.

From 1978 on, the Lambeth Conference asked that human sexuality be studied by the churches of the Communion, and this topic has been on its agenda since that time. The questions have been made more complicated by cultural factors: the roles of men and women in different societies, the place of homosexuals within different cultures, the legacy of colonialism, the differing authority of bishops and synods in the member churches. In Canada, in 1994–5, 2500 people participated in a study of *Hearing Diverse Voices, Seeking Common Ground*, using a study guide prepared by the national church.

From 1987 on, the Diocese of New Westminster in British Columbia studied the issue in parish and diocesan gatherings. In 1998, the synod asked the bishop to authorize the blessing of same-sex unions. Although there were increasing majorities of those in favour at each subsequent synod, the bishop withheld his consent until 2002. At that time, eight parishes in that diocese were authorized to conduct such blessings. In 2003, the Episcopal Church of the United States consecrated the Rt. Rev. Gene Robinson, a partnered gay man, as Bishop of New Hampshire.

In 2004, the Lambeth Commission on Communion, set up by the Archbishop of Canterbury and representative of many provinces of the Communion, prepared the Windsor Report to look at how authority is maintained and how decisions should be made in the Anglican Communion. The report set out the purpose and benefits of communion, looked at the way the Communion made decisions around the divisive issue of the ordination of women, and asked questions about the authority of Scripture, tradition, reason, and the episcopate. The Diocese of New Westminster and the Episcopal Church were reprimanded for their actions, and these churches were asked to express regret and to declare a moratorium on further such actions.

The report proposed the establishment of "a common Anglican Covenant which would make explicit and forceful the loyalty and bonds of affection which govern the relationship between the churches of the Communion." Such a covenant could deal with the relationships of communion, the exercise of autonomy, and the management of disputes when they arise. One concern about the development of a Covenant, to which all Provinces would be asked to subscribe, is that it seems to represent a growing centralization of authority in the Communion – a centralization that has not been part of our life to this time. Will this centralization impose on the Communion a uniformity that has not previously been required?

The report was forwarded to all parts of the Communion for discussion. A working group prepared a Covenant that was distributed to all Provinces in 2009. Each Province will consider its adoption through its own appropriate processes. You can find a copy of the Covenant on the website of the Anglican Communion. The Anglican Church of Canada is in the process of discussing the proposed Covenant.

21

What challenges face the Anglican Church today?

These are challenging times for the churches. All the major Christian denominations are in the middle of exploration and change, as we try to understand what it means to be a Christian in Canadian society in the 21st century.

When I speak or write on this subject, I often use the image of "the Time Being" – an image from a poem by the English author W. H. Auden. The poem, subtitled "A Christmas Oratorio," is a parable that explores the mystery of the Incarnation. What happens when the eternal meets the temporal? What does it mean for the eternal word to be made flesh?

Because the doctrine of the Incarnation is so central to our Anglican theology, it feels like a very Anglican poem. The image of living in "the Time Being" comes at the end of the poem. The child has been born, the angels and the shepherds have visited, Herod and the soldiers have acted, the Holy Family has fled to Egypt. The narrator sees that the excitement of Christmas is over. Now we must take up again the everyday threads of our lives. We must live in "the time being," between the Coming of Jesus and what many call the Second Coming, the ultimate conclusion.

We recognize this in our liturgical year. The period after Christmas and following the Easter season is called Ordinary Time in our service books. We live in the Time Being, "the most trying time of all." Auden says that we need to redeem that time from insignificance. For us,

...the time is noon:
When the Spirit must practise his scales of rejoicing.

I think that we are in the Time Being in many areas of our lives.

What are some of the challenges, and how can we face them? Here are some that I see. You may want to add others to the list.

- Canada is in a period of defining its identity.
- Our economic system seems uncertain.
- Church attendance/membership is down.
- Church members are aging.
- Church no longer seems to hold the influential position in society that it once did.
- Life in the church is not as straightforward as it once seemed.

Changing times

I think we need to acknowledge that we are in a period of change in the church, as well as in other areas of our daily lives. We have memories of a prosperous time, when churches were full of young families, when church membership was an important part of being a "pillar of the community," when there was money for church projects, when rural communities were vibrant and lively, when liturgy seemed to be fixed and unchanging.

We can never go back to the way things were. Change always moves us forward. But I think that there are some ways to respond to change that will help us move through the changes more gracefully.

We need first of all to acknowledge that things have changed and to grieve for what we have lost. As Anglicans, there are things that were important to us in church life that will never come back. We need some time to mourn this loss.

But we need to see change as a positive opportunity. We can be more intentional about planning for change. What can be changed, and what cannot? Which battles are worth fighting? And how are they best fought? Every change, no matter how small, creates new dynamics, new relationships. Every new member in a congregation, in an ACW group, or on a committee will bring about changes in that group. We need to develop a positive attitude to change, to see it as an opportunity so that we can develop our imaginations and stretch our vision of what is possible.

Any change is risky. Risk brings with it some losses – loss of control over the future, loss of confidence, loss of security. In these times, we need to plan for change and to take risks even in uncertainty. Risk is an act of will. We **choose** to act, and we **choose** to follow God, even though there are no guarantees. To live the Christian life is to step out into the unknown with faith in God's goodness and love. As Anglicans, how can we help that happen in our church and our world?

Vision 2019

In 2010, General Synod adopted a new strategic plan, Vision 2019, to guide the church through the next decade. The plan is based on the five "marks of mission" enunciated at the Anglican Consultative Council meeting in Nigeria in 1984 and at subsequent meetings. These call on the church to

- proclaim the good news of the Kingdom;
- teach, baptize, and nurture new believers;
- respond to human needs by loving service;
- seek to transform unjust structures of society;
- strive to safeguard the integrity of creation, and sustain and renew the life of the earth.

The plan encourages work in seven priority areas:

- developing leadership education for mission, evangelism, and ministry;
- supporting ministry through the Council of the North;
- walking with indigenous peoples on a journey of healing and wholeness;
- working towards peace and justice;
- engaging young people in mutual growth for mission;
- enlivening worship;
- taking on leadership roles in the Anglican Communion and ecumenical actions.

This plan will guide the work of the church in the coming years. Improving communication, developing stewardship and financial resources, and encouraging dialogue across the diversity of the Anglican Church will be part of that process.

Liturgical change

Because worship is so important to Anglicans, and because we learn our faith through the liturgy, any liturgical change is threatening. But any reading of church history indicates that the Christian church as a whole, and the Anglican Church in particular, have been very different at different periods of history. *The Book of Common Prayer*, so frequently referred to as a single unchanging document, has in fact appeared in many versions, some of which presented distinctly different theological viewpoints. In our own day, we talk as though no change occurred until *The Book of Alternative Services* appeared on the scene in 1985. Yet, within the 20th century, Canadian Anglicans used three different editions of *The Book of Common Prayer*, three or four different hymn books, and countless trial liturgies. Whatever made us think that things would stay the same? The Faith Worship and Ministry committee of the national church has prepared some principles for liturgical revision to guide changes in patterns of worship. You can find these on the website of the Anglican Church of Canada.

Liturgical change has not been confined to our own church. It is part of a worldwide movement for liturgical renewal within Anglican churches all around the world, and within many other denominations. This liturgical study and renewal continues as we explore ways to express our understanding of God in our own time and culture. Our relationship of Full Communion with the Evangelical Lutheran Church in Canada commits us to work together in liturgical renewal and revision.

Just as it is important to educate people for change, it is also important to help people to understand why our liturgical expressions change. So Anglicans need to learn more about how our worship developed and why changes are being suggested. But I think that it is also important to recognize that in this, as in other areas of life, we cannot go back and wish the changes undone. Anglicans tolerate a diversity of liturgical practice within the bounds of the authorized texts. I hope that we celebrate this diversity.

The role of women

In the last 35 years, we have seen a major change in the life of our church through the ordination of women. These decisions, and the early years of the ministry of ordained women, were very difficult for some Anglicans. But we have come through that period and can now celebrate the great gifts ordained women bring to the church.

Lay women also have come to take a more prominent role in the life of the Anglican Church. At one time the government of the church – in parish, diocesan, and national structures – was exclusively in the hands of men. But in the last 50 years, a significant number of lay women have taken positions of responsibility as wardens, vestry members, committee members, and members of synods. Lay women teach theology, do education in parishes, serve as chaplains and pastoral visitors, and assist in the liturgy.

We can celebrate this aspect of our life as a denomination and continue to work for the greater acceptance of all people in the life of our church.

An aging church

As we look around many of our parishes, we see that the age of our members is quite high. While some parishes have many young families, others do not. Sports programs, children's lessons and activities, and pressures of work all place demands on family time and energy, and may leave little time for church involvement. One of the challenges of the coming years will be to involve families in parish life in ways that are helpful and strengthening to them. We need to be aware of and employ new technologies, social media, and other ways of communication as they emerge.

I think that we need also to find new ways to involve children and young people in our worship services, in education, in service to others.

The role of the laity

At a diocesan clergy conference, clergy were asked to gather in groups according to the decade in which they were ordained. As they talked, and as they described for each other the church at the time of their ordination, they became aware of the great changes that have occurred within this span of about 40 years.

One of the major changes in the church has been the increasing role of the laity, particularly in worship. Lay people serve at the altar, read lessons, lead the prayers, sometimes preach, sometimes conduct the worship service. Lay people also take on many responsibilities for pastoral care, baptismal or marriage preparation, and education.

As I travel around the country speaking and doing workshops, I have become aware that there is a real hunger among many lay people for serious theological education. How we provide that education and encourage the ministry of lay people, both in the church and in their daily work, will be one of the major challenges of the next decades.

New ways to do ministry

As finances and membership continue to decline, new ways of doing ministry must be found. Lay people are taking a major responsibility for maintaining the ongoing life and ministry in their parishes. We need to explore what this ministry might mean in parishes and dioceses. How do these new forms of ministry affect clergy and laity? What kinds of education and training are needed, and how can other clergy and lay people assist in this training? What kind of recognition and authorization is appropriate for new ministries?

While this discussion began in rural areas, where many parishes can no longer afford to employ full-time stipendiary clergy, there are increasing numbers of urban parishes who are faced with declining resources and a need to re-examine how ministry is done. I think that the exploration of new forms of ministry will continue to be a major focus for the church in the coming years.

New national structures

As with all Christian denominations, the Anglican Church of Canada has suffered from a decline in revenue. In part, this is due to smaller numbers. In part, it is due to an economic recession with a drop in interest rates and pressure on the disposable income of parishioners. One challenge we are facing is stewardship education – how to encourage our members to give responsibly to support the work of the church. But another challenge is how to restructure the organization of the church in order to reflect the drop in our revenue.

At the national level, the church struggles with decisions about how ministry can be done most effectively with the money we have. These decisions will bring changes in the way work is done at the national level. Perhaps more programs will need to be done on the regional level, or in dioceses and parishes. These changes will inevitably bring a sense of loss but can also bring us the opportunity to reflect on the work of the church in new and imaginative ways. I hope that we can see this as an opportunity to meet the challenge creatively.

Ethical issues

We face many complex ethical issues today. New medical technology requires ethical decision-making on new issues. We continue to reflect on issues of human sexuality. We strive to make the church a welcoming and inclusive place. There are environmental issues to be considered. We continue to work for justice for all, and peace in a divided world. We live in a largely secular society. What is our responsibility as Christians in that society? These are continuing challenges that the church must face.

Anglican identity

As I have commented repeatedly throughout this book, it is difficult to define the precise details of Anglican identity. In a time of religious pluralism, it will be important for us to continue to work at exploring Anglican identity and theology. I think that it is important for us also to articulate the positive optimistic theology which I believe characterizes Anglicanism.

The dark theology that stresses the sinfulness of humans, and urges people to separate themselves from the evil world disturbs me. As an Anglican, I would like to affirm that God's creation is good, that we are placed in it to live as responsible members of society, and that we are sustained by God's grace in our daily lives. We need to articulate our Anglican way of doing theology and let that distinctive voice be heard.

Ecumenism

We need to find new ways of working together with Christians of other denominations. It is easy for us to pray for Christian unity, but the unity we seek can only come if many of our present ways and attitudes change.

We need to learn together with all Canadians what it means to live in a multicultural and multi-faith society.

Education for all

Finally, as an educator, I think one of biggest challenges will be to find effective ways of educating Anglicans. I think that many Anglicans are seeking a deeper understanding of their faith. They are looking for training to equip them to carry out their ministry in everyday life. Theological colleges and lay training centres are looking for new ways to train men and women for ministry in our church. We need to continue to explore the needs of children and young people in our churches. Everything we do in the church has an educational component. One of our challenges will be to become more intentional about the way we educate people for change and growth.

This is a time of change and uncertainty. But I believe it also to be a time of great challenge and promise. It is an exciting time to be an Anglican and to share with others in the life of this church.

Glossary of Terms

Altar: the table where the Eucharist is celebrated. The altar is placed in a central position as the focus of our worship.

Altar Guild: a group of people who see that everything is cleaned and made ready for the celebration of the Eucharist. Sometimes called a Chancel Guild.

Anglican Church of Canada: an autonomous (self-governing) church or Province within the Anglican Communion.

Anglican Communion: a family of 44 regional, national, and member churches including 34 self-governing Provinces. They share common origins in the Church of England, worship according to *The Book of Common Prayer* and other authorized texts, have an episcopal form of government, and are in communion with the Archbishop of Canterbury.

Anglican Consultative Council: a body of bishops, priests, and lay representatives of the Province of the Anglican Communion. They meet every three years in different parts of the Communion to discuss matters of common concern.

Archbishop: a title given to Metropolitans and the Primate. They are addressed in writing as "the Most Reverend," and are called "Archbishop" or "Your Grace."

Archdeaconry: a geographical subdivision of a diocese under the oversight of an Archdeacon, a senior priest appointed by the bishop to assist in supervisory and administrative tasks.

Articles: the 39 Articles of Religion, adopted in 1559 as a balanced statement of the Anglican position on a number of disputed topics.

Bishop: a priest chosen by the diocese to be ordained as bishop and to have authority and pastoral care of the diocese. In the House of Bishops, all Canadian bishops meet together to discuss issues and concerns, and to formulate guidelines governing the life of the church. A **coadjutor** bishop is one who will become the next diocesan bishop upon the retirement of the present bishop.

Suffragan, assistant, and **area** bishops assist the diocesan bishop and may have responsibility for a particular area of the diocese, but do not automatically become the next diocesan bishop. Bishops are addressed in writing as "The Right Reverend" and are called "Bishop" or "My Lord."

Canon: 1. An honorary title granted to a senior priest or an outstanding lay person. 2. A law of the church, governing its life and discipline. There are diocesan, provincial, and national canons. Canon Law is the term given to the legal inter-pretation of the canons.

Cathedral: the church where the bishop's chair or "cathedra" (the symbol of the bishop's role as chief pastor in the diocese) is located. The cathedral is often the setting for special diocesan services and is in some sense the "mother church" of the diocese.

Ceremonial: rituals and customs that add meaning to our worship. These may include making the sign of the cross, bowing to acknowledge the altar, processions around the church, the lighting of candles on the Advent wreath. These customs may vary from congregation to congregation.

Chalice: the large cup in which the wine is consecrated and served at Communion.

Chancel: in traditional architecture, the part of the church where the choir is located.

Chancellor: the senior lay officer of Synod, who is a lawyer or judge and who advises the bishop and synod on canon and civil law.

Chaplain: a priest or lay person authorized for a particular ministry of pastoral care. There are chaplains in schools, hospitals, and nursing homes, and in the Armed Services.

Churchwarden: senior lay officer of a congregation. In some dioceses, a warden is elected by the congregation and called the People's Warden; another is appointed by the incumbent and is often called the Rector's Warden. In other dioceses, the members of the congregation elect all wardens. There are two or more wardens in a parish.

Clergy: the ordained members of the church (bishops, priests, and deacons).

Collect: short prayers said by the priest or people, usually one sen-tence long, with an address to God, a petition or request, and an expression of praise. These prayers "collect" up the thoughts and prayers of the worshippers.

There is a collect for each Sunday and feast day of the church year, as well as fixed collects in the liturgy. Some collects are very old; some were written more recently.

Communicant: any baptized person who has been admitted to the Eucharist and normally attends worship in an Anglican Church.

Companion Diocese: dioceses in different parts of the Anglican world that covenant together in a special relationship of mutual interest and support (similar to the twinning of cities). Many Canadian dioceses have a companion diocese relationship with dioceses in other parts of the world.

Congregation: members of a local Christian community. A parish may be made up of one or more congregations.

Council of General Synod: the elected body that conducts the business of the Anglican Church of Canada between General Synods.

Curate: a term sometimes used to denote a full-time assistant in a parish.

Deacon: a person ordained to a ministry of service, both in the church and in the world. A deacon assists at the Eucharist but does not preside. Some persons are ordained deacons for life. Before being ordained priest, a person must be ordained as a deacon.

Dean: usually the rector of a cathedral parish. The Dean may be given diocesan responsibilities by the bishop.

Deanery: a region within an archdeaconry within which the clergy and laity consult on matters affecting church life in their area. Meetings are convened by the Regional Dean.

Diocesan Council: the body, representative of clergy and laity, that oversees the affairs of the diocese between synods. Elected at diocesan synod.

Ecclesiastical province: a regional grouping of dioceses, presided over by a Metropolitan or Archbishop. Canada has four ecclesiastical provinces: British Columbia and Yukon, Rupert's Land, Ontario, and Canada.

Episcopal: having bishops. The Anglican Church has an episcopal form of church government. Sometimes an Anglican Province uses "episcopal" in its name – the Episcopal Church of the United States.

Font: the place where baptisms take place. Often located near the door of the church as a reminder that it is by baptism that we enter the church. Otherwise placed in a prominent position at the front of the church, symbolic of baptism's importance.

General Synod: the governing body of the Anglican Church of Canada that meets every three years. The bishop, and clergy and lay representatives from each diocese attend. General Synod employs staff at its headquarters in Toronto (Church House) to carry out its work in overseas partnerships and program support.

Incarnation: the doctrine that God chose to come into the world in human form in the birth of Jesus who lived and died as one of us. Christmas is the feast of the Incarnation.

Incumbent: a priest given charge of a parish by the bishop. Sometimes called Rector or Vicar.

Lambeth Conference: a conference of all the bishops of the Anglican Communion, held every 10 years in England. It is a consultative rather than a legislative body.

Lambeth Quadrilateral: accepted in 1888 as the essentials for a reunited Christian church. They are: the Holy Scriptures, the historic creeds (Apostles' and Nicene), the two Gospel sacraments (Baptism and Eucharist), and the historic episcopate, locally adapted.

Lay person (laity): baptized but not ordained member(s) of the congregation.

Lectern: a stand that holds the Bible, from which the lessons of the day are read. Sometimes it is in the shape of an eagle.

Lectionary: a listing of all the Bible readings for Sunday services, daily services, and special days. Both *The Book of Common Prayer* and *The Book of Alternative Services* contain lectionaries. The Anglican Church follows the three-year pattern of the *Revised Common Lectionary*, put together by an international group of scholars.

Liturgy: the ways in which Anglicans worship.

Member: a person baptized in the name of the Trinity who attends an Anglican church regularly.

Metropolitan: the presiding bishop of an ecclesiastical province. Usually called "Archbishop."

Ministers: all the baptized members of the church, who are carrying out their ministry to worship God and to serve others. Some people have special ministries: wardens, church school teachers, choir members, assistants in worship. Certain ministries in the church (bishop, priest, deacon) require that a person be ordained.

Nave: the main body of the church, where pews or chairs are located. The word means "ship," describing the church as it carries its members on their pilgrimage.

Non-stipendiary: a member of the clergy who earns a living in secular work.

Ordained: a person called, tested, and approved by the church is set apart or ordained by a bishop for special ministry as a bishop, priest, or deacon.

Parish: a geographical area in which a priest, deacon, or lay person is licensed to serve the church. A parish may be made up of one or more congregations.

Parish Council: the decision-making body in a parish, composed of elected lay members. Sometimes called a vestry.

Parishioner: a baptized person who usually worships in a parish.

Paten: the plate on which the bread rests during Communion.

Presider or Presiding Celebrant: the priest or bishop who presides at a celebration of Holy Communion.

Priest: a person ordained by a bishop for ministry of Word and Sacrament.

Primate: the chief or presiding bishop of a national church.

Province: 1. A grouping of dioceses. *See* "Ecclesiastical province." In this book, I have used lower case "p" to describe this kind of province. 2. A national church, part of the Anglican Communion. In this book, I have used a capital "P" to indicate this kind of province.

Provincial Synod: governing body of an ecclesiastical province.

Pulpit: the place from which the sermon is preached.

Reception: the act of receiving Holy Communion.

Rector: a priest to whom the bishop has designated care of a parish.

Regional Dean: a priest appointed by the bishop as chair of a Regional Deanery, with administrative and leadership responsibilities.

Regional Deanery: a geographical grouping of parishes meeting from time to time to discuss common concerns.

Sacraments: an "outward and visible sign of an inward and spiritual grace" *(BCP)*. God's grace is expressed to us through material objects. The two principle sacraments are Baptism and the Eucharist. Other lesser rites "commonly called sacraments" are Confirmation, Marriage, Ordination, Reconciliation, and Unction.

Sanctuary: the part of the church building where the altar is located.

See: the "seat" or chair of a bishop, usually in the diocesan cathedral. It is a symbol of the bishop's authority and jurisdiction.

Stole: a narrow band of fabric, in the colour of the season, worn by the clergy during the celebration of the Eucharist. Deacons wear the stole over the left shoulder. Priests wear it draped over both shoulders.

Synod: the governing body of a diocese, made up of all the licensed clergy, lay representatives of all the parishes, ex officio members, and the bishop. They meet at designated intervals to do the business of the diocese.

Vestry: 1. A room where clergy put on their vestments. 2. The decision-making body of a congregation, elected from the lay members. 3. In some parts of Canada, the annual meeting of parishioners.

Warden: *see* Churchwarden.

Bibliography

Books quoted in the text *(many of these are no longer in print)*

de Waal, Esther. *A World Made Whole*. London: Fount, 1991.

Diehl, William E. *The Monday Connection: On Being an Authentic Christian in a Weekday World*. New York: HarperCollins, 1993.

Dix, Gregory. *The Shape of the Liturgy*. Westminster: Dacre Press, 1945.

Dozier, Verna. *The Authority of the Laity*. Washington: Alban Institute, 1982.

Hanchey, Howard. *Church Growth and the Power of Evangelism*. Cambridge: Cowley, 1990.

Hearing Diverse Voices, Seeking Common Ground. Toronto: Anglican Book Centre, 1994.

Holmes, Urban T. *What is Anglicanism?* Toronto: Anglican Book Centre, 1982.

Mission in a Broken World. Anglican Consultative Council report, 1990.

Sykes, Stephen. "The Incarnation as the Foundation of the Church." *Incarnation and Myth: The Debate Continued*. ed. Michael Goulder. London: SCM, 1979.

Westerhoff, Caroline A. *Calling: A Song for the Baptized*. Cambridge: Cowley, 1994.

Suggestions for further reading

Bartlett, Alan. *A Passionate Balance: The Anglican Tradition*. London: Darton, Longman and Todd, 2007.

Baycroft, John. *The Anglican Way*. Toronto: Anglican Book Centre, 1980.

Bays, Patricia. *Anglican Diversity*. Toronto: Anglican Book Centre, 2001.

———. *Meet the Family*. (revised) Wood Lake Books and Anglican Book Centre, 2012

Chapman, Mark. *Anglicanism: A Very Short Introduction*. Oxford: Oxford University Press, 2007.

Chapman, Raymond. *Means of Grace, Hope of Glory: Five Hundred Years of Anglican Thought*. Norwich: Canterbury Press, 2005.

Countryman, L. William. *The Poetic Imagination: An Anglican Spiritual Tradition*. Maryknoll: Orbis Books, 1999.

For All the Saints: Prayers and Readings for Saints' Days. Compiled by Stephen Reynolds. Toronto: Anglican Book Centre, 1994.

Greer, Rowan A. *Anglican Approaches to Scripture, from the Reformation to the Present.* New York: Crossroad, 2006.

Kitch, Anne E. *The Anglican Family Prayer Book.* Toronto: ABC Publishing, 2004.

Life in the Eucharist. Toronto: Anglican Book Centre, 1986.

Love's Redeeming Work: The Anglican Quest for Holiness. Compiled by Geoffrey Rowell, Kenneth Stevenson, and Rowan Williams. Oxford: Oxford University Press, 2001.

Murray, K. D. *From a Long Perspective: The Foundational Documents, Ecumenical Covenants, and Other Significant Agreements of the Anglican Church of Canada.* Toronto: ABC Publishing, 2007.

Quinn, Frederick. *To Be a Pilgrim: The Anglican Ethos in History.* New York: Crossroad, 2001.

Schmidt, Richard H. *Glorious Companions: Five Centuries of Anglican Spirituality.* Grand Rapids: William B. Eerdmans, 2002.

Webber, Christopher. *Give Us Grace: An Anthology of Anglican Prayers.* Harrisburg: Morehouse Publishing, 2004.

Williams, Rowan. *Anglican Identities.* Cambridge: Cowley Publications, 2003.

Websites

The Anglican Church of Canada, www.anglican.ca

The Anglican Communion, www.anglicancommunion.org

Anglicans Online, www.anglicansonline.org

Anglican Church Women, www.acwcanada.com

Mothers Union, www.mothersunioncanada.ca

The Primate's World Relief and Development Fund, www.pwrdf.org

Canadian Council of Churches, www.ccc-cce.ca

World Council of Churches, www.oikoumene.org

Young Anglicans, www.generation.anglican.ca

Ask and Imagine, www.askandimagine.org

Study Guide by Jim Taylor

Purpose

Let's be clear about the purpose for these sessions. It's to help people feel they belong to this community of people, this denomination, this church. It is not to transfer a dump truck full of information into their minds. So there are no correct answers to memorize, no tests to pass, no diplomas to hand out.

Many people recall their school years as a time of having to give the right answer. If they didn't have the right answer, it was wiser to keep their mouths shut. In church and in faith, right or wrong answers don't apply. Everyone – clergy, leaders, and lay participants – is on a journey of faith and growth together.

If, at the end of this time together, participants feel comfortable with one another and with what this church believes and does, the course will have been a success.

Learning principles

Adults learn best by association. They test the new information they receive against what they already know from their own experience. If it fits, they keep it, and it becomes an integral part of the person. If it doesn't fit – or if there's no experience they can fit it to – they will soon forget it and lose it.

A key element of adult education, then, is to help participants identify experiences to which they can connect the new ideas. Probably the best way to do this is through small group discussion. As people tell their own stories to each other, they bring their own experience out into the open. They have something to connect their learning to.

A lecture may allow a speaker to present a lot of information, but it doesn't give the learners the opportunity to assimilate that information, to integrate it with their most valuable resource – their own experience.

A group could be anything from two to eight persons. The larger the group, the more time it takes to involve everyone in discussing an idea. More than eight people and the group is likely to split into two. There will either be separate discussions, or some who do all the talking and some who just listen. Those who "just listen" without contributing may never make the effort to find, in the library of their own experiences, the foundations on which to build their faith.

And because those foundations are experiences, there can be no right or wrong answers. One participant cannot say to another, "That wasn't what happened," or "Your experience was wrong." It's possible to offer an alternative experience or a different interpretation of an experience, but not to challenge the experience itself. Life stories tend to evoke sympathy and compassion; judgment and disagreement usually result from generalized statements of principle or conviction.

Therefore we recommend
- using small groups
- involving everyone
- encouraging storytelling.

Atmosphere

Because many adults (especially those over 40) may have painful memories of their school years, it's important to make the room itself feel friendly. Avoid, as far as possible, setups that look like a traditional classroom. Set chairs in a circle, or at least in a semi-circle – much as people would naturally sit in a living room, for example. Prefer comfortable chairs to uncomfortable ones.

Supply tea and coffee, juice, and cookies if you wish, and encourage people to help themselves. A bit of food and drink loosens things up. But don't let refreshments become a burden, where the suppliers feel they have to top the previous week's provisions.

Don't put anyone under pressure. If people don't want to join in small group discussion, don't force them. Participation must always be voluntary.

Ask participants to agree to treat anything they hear in the sessions as confidential.

Leadership

Leaders set the style for everyone else.

Many people hesitate to share their own stories and experiences with others. They may fear laughter, or ridicule, or misunderstanding, or they may have been taught not to talk about themselves. Leaders willing to risk being vulnerable, by including a few of their own experiences as illustrations or examples, model the desired style for others.

At the same time, leaders should not be so personal as to draw all the attention to themselves. That models a style that encourages other participants to dominate discussion, and may suggest that everyone else's faith journey is secondary.

Having a variety of people take leadership sets a good example for others. A leadership team (rather than a "lone wolf" doing everything) encourages community among participants. The leadership team should meet well in advance, practice among themselves the principles of the program, and divide up responsibilities for each session.

Remember that participants often know less about their faith and their church than they like to admit. Churchy language may baffle, or worse, alienate them. Explain church-related words and ideas, or better yet, use a story or personal anecdote to give these words meaning in context.

Since the purpose is to help people belong, not to get through a specified curriculum, leaders should not allow an agenda to dominate the sessions, other than to ensure that sessions start and end on time. When participants want to discuss a point, that's much more important than moving on just because a schedule says it's time.

Use questions, not authority, to direct or focus the discussion. Simple questions – sometimes even silly questions! – almost always stimulate discussion much better than complex ones. Avoid "closed" questions that ask for yes/no or right/wrong answers (unless you want to cut off discussion); use "open-ended" questions that ask for feelings or experiences.

Bibles

It's always a good idea for each member to have a Bible. (How much you use the Bible, in each session, will depend on the theological temperature of your congregation, but it's never a mistake to have Bibles available.) Encourage participants to use one of the modern translations: the New Revised Standard Version, the New Jerusalem Bible, the New International Version. The old King James Version is a treasured part of our religious heritage, but the English language has changed so much since it was published four centuries ago that its wordings are as likely to conceal meaning as to reveal it. We recommend a study Bible, either the *HarperCollins Study Bible* or the *New Oxford Annotated Bible*, for those wanting to explore texts more deeply.

Typical format of a session

1. **Informal gathering time:** People are free to stand around and chat.
2. **Opening:** 5–10 minutes to reduce tension and get people comfortable with one another. Familiar songs can do this; so can simple exercises and activities related to the theme of the session.
3. **Input:** By expressing the message of a chapter in his or her own words, a leader introduces participants to the theme for the evening and gets them thinking. About 15 minutes maximum. Remember that this is not a sermon opportunity.
4. **Brainstorming:** A short period, perhaps 5 minutes, which encourages people to bring forth ideas and reactions without fear of contradiction or challenge.
5. **Discussion:** in small groups, of suggested questions for about 30 minutes.
6. **Feedback:** Responses from small groups – not reports of what they discussed, but of what they learned from each other and, perhaps, what difference this will make in their lives. 10–15 minutes, depending on the size of group.
7. **Closing:** Inform participants of chapters they should read for the next session. Then follow with prayer or music. Keep it brief: 2–3 minutes.

The number and timing of sessions

This study guide suggests five sessions, each running approximately 90 minutes. There's nothing magic about the number five – you might choose to do fewer sessions, or you might choose to use the pattern here to create additional sessions, based on other chapters in the book.

The sessions could be held on a series of evenings. Or you could, without much adapting, run them over a weekend, from Friday evening to Sunday afternoon.

Session 1 (Chapters 1 and 2)
Who are we, anyway?

Opening: Welcome the participants. Explain anything necessary about confidentiality, getting coffee, cleaning up, etc.

Lead in an opening prayer, such as the following:

O God, you have chosen and called us to be your people. You have made us members of your church. Give us a sense of who we are, so that we can live more effectively as your witnesses to the world. Bless your church. Keep it focused clearly on the good news of Jesus Christ, and let it be a place where all are warmly welcomed and included in your community of joy, peace, and love. Amen.

Opening activity: Do one or more of the following.

a) sing a song or hymn to gather people together.

b) make up name tags that show
 – the person's name
 – the person's origin (place, country, former denomination if applicable)

c) ask people, in groups of 2–4, to talk about their earliest memories of church or Sunday school. What makes those experiences particularly memorable? Remember that not everyone will have attended church or Sunday school as a child. For some, their "earliest memories" will be quite recent.

Input: A leader (not necessarily clergy) who has read the book and distilled the main points of Chapters 1 and 2, talks about what makes this congregation in this denomination special for him or her. Highlight or underline not more than six quotations in the chapters that are likely to provoke discussion. You don't have to agree with them all – in fact, it's good if the leader doesn't agree with everything in the book, as that frees the participants also to find their own viewpoints – but do not choose quotations simply to dispute them!

If you wish to include a biblical base, look first at the lectionary readings for this week, to see if any of them offer insights. Alternatively, consider 1 Peter 2:9–10 or Deuteronomy 7:6–8.

Brainstorming: Invite participants to call out what makes this congregation in this denomination special for them. Encourage people to volunteer ideas quickly.

Remember that in brainstorming, no one is ever right or wrong – if one person likes this congregation for its conservative theology, and another for its liberal theology, they're both right. Put both answers up! The purpose of this brainstorming is not to reach any kind of consensus, or even to identify any common themes (though it's nice if they appear) but to set up an expectation that anyone can present any idea.

Have someone write the suggestions up quickly on a board or flipchart for future reference, if necessary.

Discussion: If there are eight or more people, divide into sub-groups. Ask each group to discuss questions such as these:
- What kinds of people does this congregation particularly attract?
- What stories do you know about the origins of this congregation?
- Who do you think of as a dominant influence in shaping the faith/ theology of this congregation? What do you know about him/her?
- What does it mean to you to be "a chosen race, a royal priesthood... God's own people"? (1 Peter 2:9)

> **Tip:** Leaders of discussion groups are there to keep discussion moving and to prevent any individuals from dominating. As far as possible, discourage people from citing memorized Bible verses or doctrinal assertions, as these tend to cut off any further discussion. If such responses do occur, ask a supplementary question, such as, "Was there some particular time in your life when that message took on particular meaning for you?"

Feedback: Not a report on what was discussed, but what was learned from the discussion. Some people may want to share individual insights; others may want to identify some (often vague) emerging consensus.

Closing: Depending on time and the inclinations of the group, close with a suitable song and/or prayer. Invite people to consume the last of the refreshments. Don't hurry people out – some of the most valuable discussion may take place after the formal part of the session is over.

Session 2 (Chapters 3, 11, 12)
Our ways of worshipping

Because this session focuses on patterns and practices of worship, you might want to invite your priest(s) and a member of the worship committee (or its equivalent) to attend this session. You may find it useful to have copies of *The Book of Common Prayer (BCP)* and *The Book of Alternative Services (BAS)* available for reference.

Opening: Distribute name tags again. If you didn't use denominational origin last time, add it to the name tag this time.

Do one or more of the following to get people talking about their experience of worship in church:

a) Do a chain interview. Set up two rows of chairs, enough for everyone present, facing each other. Hand out sheets that contain questions such as these:
- When did you first begin to attend church services?
- How were you welcomed?
- At what point did you begin to feel that you belonged?
- How old were you when you were baptized?
- When did you first receive Communion?
- If you attended church as a child, what used to make you fidget most?
- As a child, did you go to church Sunday morning, or Sunday evening, or ...?
- What else was there to do on Sunday?
- How did you get to church?
- How did they keep the church warm in winter?
- What hymns do you remember singing?
- How much did you put in the offering plate in those days?
- How has your life been influenced by the clergy you have known?
- What friendships influenced your coming to church?
- Have you made new friends through your life in the church?
- Have you been to church in another country? What impressed you about that experience?

There should be at least as many questions as people. Have the people sit on the chairs, facing each other. They ask each other the first question, and note their answers. Then everyone moves one seat to the right, and asks the next question of the person now facing them, and so on, until you run out of time or all questions have been answered.

b) In groups of three or four – but never individually – have people create a mural representing worship as they remember it from their childhood. For those who did not attend church as children, input for the mural can be from the church they attend now, or churches they have attended as an adult. It doesn't matter if the group can't agree enough to produce a finished piece of art; the task is simply an excuse to get people visualizing their early worship context. Provide any supplies needed: newsprint, crayons, coloured markers, magazines, glue...

c) Music, preferably familiar pieces whose words or tunes lend themselves to the theme of this session.

Input: One or more members of the leadership team (which can include participants) who have read the book and distilled the main points of Chapters 3, 11 and 12, talks about how this congregation in this denomination typically worships.

Highlight or underline up to six quotations in the chapters that are likely to provoke discussion. It's helpful to choose references that may have been new insights for you, or that reinforced previous understandings. Remember that this is not a learned lecture – it's a way of sharing what makes worship special and meaningful for you.

If you wish to include a biblical base, look first at the lectionary readings for this week to see if any offer insights. Alternatively, consider Psalms 96, 98, or 100; or Exodus 20:8–11; from the New Testament, Acts 20:7 describing the believers meeting on the first day of the week rather than the Sabbath, or 1 Corinthians 11:23–26 describing the central ritual of Christian worship.

Brainstorming: Invite the participants to call out all the questions they ever had about worship, but never had the courage to ask. Write them up on a board or flipchart for further reference. At this time, don't attempt to answer the questions – simply identify them. Treat all questions seriously, no matter how trivial some may seem.

Discussion – in small groups: Invite the groups to select three or four questions from the list for discussion. See what responses they can generate from

- their own wisdom and experience
- the book
- the expertise of the priests and worship committee members.

If necessary, supplement the questions listed by the group with other questions such as these:

- If you had to shorten a service, what part(s) would you cut? Why?
- What kind of role do laypeople play in our congregation's worship?
- How often do we celebrate Communion (or the Eucharist, the Mass, or the Lord's Supper)? Why do we follow that practice?
- What is the oldest (or most historic) component in our worship services?
- What do you think God might consider "a joyful noise unto the Lord"?

Feedback: Ask what people have learned about their worship services during this session. What surprised them? What requires further thought? These questions may suggest a need for future parish programs on worship-related subjects.

Closing: Assign the chapters for the next session. Invite someone to give at the next session a presentation about how they live their Christian life from Monday to Saturday. Close with prayer, or music, or both.

Session 3 (Chapters 4, 5, and 8)
The rest of the week

Opening: Distribute name tags. Introduce any newcomers to the old-timers, and vice versa.

Do the following, depending on time and interest:

    a) Distribute sheets of paper. Issue a challenge – see who can create the longest list of church or community organizations that the members of this group are active in. The list maker should not include his or her own activities and associations – the point is to learn about others' involvement. When time is up, share the lists, wonder about the number of organizations and causes this congregation supports in one way or another, and give a round of applause to the person who gathered the longest list. (Note: it can be interesting to identify the church-related activities in the total list, to see to what extent the congregation's interests are focused inward or outward.)

    b) Now that people have identified the organizations to which they and others belong, form a "common link" chain. Each person joins hands with someone in a similar organization. (So a hockey coach who has subscription tickets to the symphony might join with a hockey parent on one side and a high school music teacher on the other.) Remember that each person has two hands, and probably a dozen or more possible links. The idea is to get everyone connected to someone else. Expect bedlam as people make and break the chain to accommodate others and get a maximum of people involved.

    c) Appropriate music.

Input: For about 10 minutes, have a presentation from one of the group on what it means to them to be a Christian during the rest of the week, Monday through Saturday. How does that person live his or her faith in the daily dilemmas of work and family and leisure? Again, a few good, provocative quotations from the book will help, but don't let the talk become simply a summary of the book.

    To incorporate biblical teaching, first check the lectionary readings for the week. If those don't relate well, try Micah 6:8 or 1 Corinthians 12:4–27.

Brainstorming: In a church group, some people may be hesitant to say what they personally think of the church. But they'll almost always be able to say what they think others are saying about the church!

    Ask: "What do people say about the church – the Christian church in general, and this church in particular?" Write the comments on a board or flipchart.

Tip: When fielding "brainstormed" ideas, watch out for persistent trends. That is, if all the comments are positive, you might need to say, "Aren't there people who claim the church is full of hypocrites?" or "What about the claim that the church is always asking for money?" Similarly, if the trend seems to emphasize negative aspects of the church, plant ideas that may generate some positive responses: "What do they say about our Food Bank?" or "I've heard that people love our choir."

Discussion: Using the book, Chapter 8, identify and list the social issues on which your church has taken a stand. Do not discuss them yet – just list them.

Have each small group (if you have divided into small groups) choose one issue they would like to discuss in more depth. As well as considering the biblical or theological rationale for that stand, compare how that stand relates to the attitudes about the church that were identified in the brainstorming period. (For example, if the issue chosen is "remarriage of divorced persons," compare that to a perception of the church as, say, "a closed and exclusive club.")

Feedback: Ask people to identify what they found comforting about this session's discussion, and what they found disturbing.

Closing: Assign chapters to read for the next session. Close with music or prayer or both.

Session 4 (Chapter 7; also 3, 11, and 12)
What we believe

Please note: this session does not attempt to define what any person or congregation should believe. It intends merely to help participants identify what they believe, and to see how those beliefs fit together in a congregational pattern.

Opening: Name tags. Introduce any newcomers.

Put out some jigsaw puzzles on tables before the session. Invite early arrivers to play with the puzzles. Children's puzzles – perhaps borrowed from the Sunday school – can be done relatively quickly and cleared away. Avoid complicated puzzles that will distract people's attention from the session itself.

Do one or more of the following:

a) Appropriate music to build community.

b) The three principles of Anglican theology are Scripture, tradition, and reason. Designate one area in the room for each of these principles. Invite people to move to the area that represents for them the primary source of authority. There is no right or wrong. For each of us, there is a time when one aspect or another is more dominant in our thinking. This may be the first time some people have identified themselves by their theology. Invite some feedback as the group sits for the Input section.

c) Hand out a sheet with a number of metaphors for God listed on it, such as the following. Make sure there's a good mix of metaphors. Ask people to rank those metaphors according to their own preferences, and then to compare their rankings with at least one other person.

- A mother hen with her chicks (Matthew 23:37, Luke 13:34)
- A king crowned and sitting on a throne (Isaiah 66:1, Hebrews 12:2)
- A mighty wind (John 3:8, Acts 2:2)
- A fire raging out of control (Exodus 3:2, Acts 2:3)
- A still small voice (1 Kings 19:12–13)
- A mighty and victorious conqueror (Psalms 24:8)
- A farmer sowing seeds (Matthew 13:3–8)
- An eagle soaring above the earth (Exodus 19:4)
- The owner of a vineyard (Mark 12:1–11)
- A thief in the night (Luke 12:39–40, 1 Thessalonians 5:2)
- A woman cleaning her house (Luke 15:8–10)
- The welcoming father (Luke 15:11–32)
- A judge (Genesis 18:25, John 5:30)
- A spouse discovering a partner's adultery (Hosea 2:2)
- The host of a banquet (Luke 14:16–24)
- A gardener pruning vines (Isaiah 5:3–5, John 15:1–2)
- A potter working clay (Jeremiah 18:6)
- A person doing laundry (Psalms 51:7, Acts 22:16)

Note: The intent is to discuss the metaphors, not to look them up. Biblical sources are given here only for reference, in case anyone challenges a metaphor's legitimacy.

Input: This talk probably comes as close to a traditional lecture as any. Someone needs to go over Chapters 3 and 7, identifying "turning points" in the shaping of the faith to which this congregation belongs. Who were some of the key figures? Why were they significant? What difference do they still make to us today? However, the speaker doing the summarizing should try to avoid sounding like an authority; he or she should admit, "Until I read this book, I hadn't realized that..." or "I realize I hadn't thought much about..."

For a biblical emphasis, check first the lectionary readings for the week; or consider 1 Corinthians 1:22–25, Isaiah 55:6–9, Deuteronomy 6:4–5 (with Matthew 22:37, Mark 12:29–30, or Luke 10:27).

Brainstorming: Ask people to develop a "job description" for an absolutely ideal member of this church. What would that person have to do? What would that person have to believe? Don't worry if some of the responses are contradictory – write them on the board or flipchart anyway.

Try to keep people out of self-imposed ruts. If all the comments deal with church activities, ask, "What about his/her family life?" If the comments lean to the financial side, ask, "Doesn't anyone need a Sunday school teacher?" If the requirements all tend to be exclusively practical, ask, "So this person doesn't have to believe in God?"

Discussion: in your group(s), do one or both of the following:
  a) Try to narrow the list of "job requirements" down to no more than a half-dozen points. Discuss how those are biblically or traditionally sound – or why the Bible and tradition don't apply in this instance.
  b) Discuss questions such as these:
   • What does it feel like to fall head-over-heels in love? Have you ever felt that way about God?
   • What kind of world did your grandparents grow up in? How different is it from your world today?

- If being Christian were a crime, would there be enough evidence to convict you?
- If the Christian faith were a treasure that could be contained in a big box, what kind of role would you play in relation to that treasure box? (Examples: guard, box polisher, scout warning of danger, prospector seeking new treasures to add, ticket seller for gawking tourists, someone handing it out to those in need, professor studying it, etc.)
- Since the Christian faith is a relationship with God and with others, what helps you to deepen and sustain those relationships?

Feedback: What have people learned about their faith and church today? What difference will it make in their lives? (Remember that it's not the facts that people have learned that matter, but their relationship to those historical facts and doctrines.)

Closing: Music and prayer are always suitable. We suggest, for this session, saying together one of the historic statements of Christian faith such as the Nicene or Apostles' Creed.

Session 5 (Chapter 6 and 18)
Commitment to ministry

This session anticipates closing with Communion or a symbolic agape meal. For that, you will need to have bread and wine prepared.

Opening: Name tags and introductions, as appropriate.

Do one or more of the following:

a) Sing again some of the songs you have used in other sessions.

b) Make up a group of name tags of fairly well-known people in the church; locally, nationally, internationally, or historically. Stick a name onto each person's back. People have to find out the name on their back by asking questions about that person's ministry. Most questions should be answerable with yes or no. The more local names you can include, the more the message that ministry is not restricted to the famous will get across.

c) Try a variant on the children's game of "whisper a message around the circle." Choose a simple sentence of six or so words – not a favourite verse from the Bible. Say it to the first person in the circle, so that everyone can hear it. That person changes just one word in that sentence and passes it on to the next person. No one may repeat a change that someone else made already.

An example might go like this:

- I love pickles on my hamburgers.
- I hate pickles on my hamburgers.
- I hate pickles on your hamburgers.
- I hate pickles on your raincoat.
- You hate pickles on your raincoat.

The point, if anyone doesn't get it, is how each person's contribution, though it may seem small, affects the message.

Input: With reference to Chapters 6 and 18 (and perhaps also Chapter 5), try to identify the particular ministry that you feel God is calling this congregation, in this place, at this time, in this denomination, to perform. Admit that this is your view, and that others may not agree. Include some stumbling blocks and potholes that may prevent this congregation from accomplishing its ministry.

Remember that you're not talking about someone "out there," but about the ministry of these people, right here, right now, who have studied and struggled with you for the last five sessions.

For biblical connections, check the lectionary passages for this week, or see Mark 1:16–20, Romans 12:3–8, Jeremiah 31:31–34, Luke 4:17–20, or Luke 8:1–3.

Brainstorming: What other ideas can people come up with to identify the ministry of this congregation, in this place, with these resources, at this time? Include the ideas presented during the Input part of the program. (Remember to list all ideas, no matter how unlikely, and do not allow anyone to argue with any of the ideas offered. If someone doesn't like a suggestion, invite them to offer an alternate.)

Discussion: In your group(s), discuss questions such as these:
- What is a ministry?
- Who has a ministry?
- Who ministers to me? How?
- What is my ministry to others? How do I engage in it?

Feedback: Instead of asking for feedback in the usual way, ask everyone to take five minutes in silence, look at the ideas on the board or flipchart, choose just one item from that list where they can make a difference, and commit themselves to start making that difference. Have each person write that commitment on a slip of paper, for use in the closing act of worship.

Closing: If you have a Communion service or agape meal, bring in the elements. Remind people that historically, these elements were gifts from the people's own fields and orchards. Suggest that along with these symbolic gifts, we need to add our real and present commitments.

As part of the service, formal or informal, invite each person in turn to place the slip of paper with his or her commitment on it on the table beside the bread and wine. Those who are willing could read out their commitment, thus going public with it.

Close with a Communion prayer, or a prayer such as this:

Gracious God, we thank you for the time we have shared together in this study of our faith. Continue to work in us, to make us the people you have chosen us to be. Give us opportunities for ministry, as you see fit. Equip us to serve you faithfully and well, and give us joy in our service. Enable us to trust you, always, in what you have done for us and all people through Jesus. Amen.

Credits: prayers and some Bible readings by Kenn Ward; other readings and activities suggested by Bev Milton, Norma Lang, and Marilyn Perry.